CATALYZE

BEAT THE EXCUSES, REDEEM YOUR TIME AND
ACTIVATE YOUR CHILDREN'S DESTINY THROUGH
PRAYER AND PROPHECY

Catalyze
© 2021 Franca Atokolo

Except otherwise stated, all Scripture references are from the New King James Version.

ISBN: 9798595319348

Published by:
Hesed House Publishing,
Abuja-Nigeria.

Printed in Nigeria by:
Unicorn Technology
+2347034847370, +2348054491782

Cover Concept: Fiona Peters Intl
fionapetersintl@gmail.com
+2347037753506

TABLE OF CONTENTS

DEDICATION

To my Jewels Natasha, Havilah, and Victor- three of the most beautiful, intelligent and interesting humans ever. Being your mum is the cutest thing that has happened to me and It's been a privilege raising you.

To Ajuma, Kate, David, Deborah and Lisa-You schooled me in motherhood in ways only your entrance into my life could have. Once a mom, always a mom. You are always in my prayers.

ACKNOWLEDGEMENT

I am deeply grateful to all the remarkable people who made their contributions to this book.

First and foremost I am eternally grateful to the author of my life, my everything, God Almighty for His love and graciousness. To the amazing person of the Holy Spirit who ignited and inspired this book, You have been a faithful Friend, Coach and Partner.

I'm thankful for my parents Late Hon. Anthony Ijika and Mrs Catherine Mariya Akoto, for raising, loving, and providing for me.

To my husband and my heartbeat, for being a shoulder to always lean on, my teacher and pastor over the years: your encouragement, your love and absolute belief in me continues to pay off. Honey, I love you forever.

I'm grateful to the mothers who were candid and real

in sharing their experiences of motherhood and delayed conception with me and other women. Mrs Omijeta Ojabo, Professor Elizabeth Amuta, Mrs Iniobong Ebong, Mrs Victoria Omale, Pastor Onyema Monye, thank you and God bless you for sharing your heart with others.

A big thanks to the entire Women of Worth Fellowship and Mothers on a Mission Support Group, who have believed the vision and walked this path with me to serve God's purpose zealously. Thank you for your love

I am indebted to the array of editors who worked tirelessly on the manuscripts to produce a finished product in the persons of: Pastor Obisike Onuoha, Apostle Victor Atokolo; Omijeta Ojabo and Pastor Steve Ojeide for the proof reading. Thank you for your patience and detailed labour to ensure this piece is readable.

I greatly appreciate all my protégés, friends, family, followers for your support and push. Thank you for setting the bar high.

Finally, to all the Mothers, with a high sense of purpose, I salute you all for your love and prayer labour over your children. Much respect to all the single Ladies who courageously and faithfully prepare through prayer, the path for their children to walk in even before they arrive. My faith and love to all women whose eyes are on Jehovah for the miracle of babies.

FOREWORD

I appreciate the honor to write this foreword because I consider the content of this book an all-time essential for every woman irrespective of their motherhood status.

It is an honor to be a mother, a co-laborer with the Creator.

Franca Atokolo has been searching for tested truth that will help raise her children well. She had once asked me what I was doing to positively impact my children. Somehow she and her husband, Rev. Atokolo know all my children and have been close to several of them. She has consulted many books including the bible that offer advice on child upbringing and sought testimonies of mothers. Her discoveries brought overwhelming success and she has decided to share her exciting knowledge with other women.

Prayer is the key... the master key. It is the spiritual weapon that does not fail. We cannot overemphasize the role of prayer in victorious living. Praying for children is a priority for every parent because Proverbs says when a child is trained in the way he should go, he will not depart from it. The Holy Spirit does the work of transformation in character and conduct in response to prayer and teaching of the Word. The enemy will resist the work of the Holy Spirit but we always have confidence for victory in Jesus' name. The depth of your prayers and patience reveals the commitment to duty, expectations, and dependence on the all-knowing God who answers prayers.

Having known Franca Atokolo for many years, and watched her unalloyed ministry alongside her husband, I am not surprised that she received the burden to labor to serve the body of Christ with this practical book. Her quest for excellence, her desire to be the best mother, and the cry in her heart for every mother to get it right in parenting are palpable throughout the pages of this book. I salute her courage and diligence and pray that the prayer life of every reader will receive fire and be transformed.

"Blessed is she who believed, for there will be a fulfillment of those things which were told her

from the Lord." Luke 1:45 NKJV

I welcome this book and recommend it wholeheartedly to all women.

Professor Elizabeth U. Amuta

It was the beginning of the year again, when my local church usually sets aside 21 days to fast and pray for the New Year. On this particular day, I had gone for the evening prayer meeting with my family as usual. I had gotten into the prayer mood and was focused on

the particular prayer point raised when suddenly, I felt an intensity in my bowels. The prayer in tongues got deeper and though, it was a spiritual encounter, I felt physical pressure as well. As I prayed more, I sensed God wanted to speak to me, so I disconnected from the general prayer for a while to listen. After some time, His clear distinct voice came through saying to me to write a book on prayer for Mums. I was startled, since the thought of writing a book on prayer had never crossed my mind before. I did not even feel qualified to take on this assignment. I quickly wrote down what He said as He gave me the sequence of the book's chapters. From that moment until I typed the last words of this book, I have experienced unusual grace, peace, and favor concerning this project.

Six months before the above encounter, I had started a Prayer Support Group offline and online for mothers. The idea came to me from a personal need to have a small circle of Mums with whom I pray together for our children. I figured out that 'two' was better than 'one', and that we could hold one another accountable to pray consistently for our kids. I also wanted to provide a platform where we could carry aspiring mothers and young mothers along on this journey of starting to pray for our children early.

I looked around and saw a lot of young failed marriages, jobless youths, young offenders, and other forms of juvenile delinquency and dysfunction. I thought that if mothers could seriously prioritize praying for their children, we will stop the enemy from having an upper hand in these children's lives. The more I pondered on this project, the clearer it became that the information in this book was a needed truth for mothers; especially for both the young mothers and for the aspiring ones.

I am convinced that this piece of truth will serve as a tool among such, to change the narrative of intentional motherhood for the next generation.

INTRODUCTION

"And she spake out with a loud voice, and said, blessed art thou among women, and blessed is the fruit of thy womb."- Luke 1:42

Nothing prepares you for motherhood, and nothing compares to it. Being a Mum has been quite an experience, an experience of a lifetime. Motherhood comes with the anxiety and curiosity of expecting a newborn - especially if it's your first: the joy of finally becoming a Mum, the challenge of adjusting to a new lifestyle, of caring for a young one who is completely dependent on you, the responsibility of nurturing and grooming your kid into a sound adult, the obligation of living up to a standard that the person you brought forth can emulate.

The status of motherhood comes with an array of demands. These demands change with each season or stage of the child's growth, but alongside all of these is the pressing and mandatory responsibilities on mothers to birth their children's destiny in prayer.

I remember when we were going to have our first baby, the news of a baby on the way was exhilarating and unnerving at the same time. It was a mixed feeling. While I was excited about the thought of having a baby for the first time, I was more scared than excited.   Two key questions plagued my mind: "Am I going to be a good mother?" "What would my baby look like?"

I realized I had control over the first question but not over the second. It then dawned on me that I was not any different from every expectant Mum who is usually curious to know who her baby would look like. I knew we were having a girl. Who she physically takes after, (whether she'll look like me or her dad (she had to look like either one of us anyway)) didn't matter as much as how she ultimately would turn out here on earth!

This reflective moment reminded me of when my husband and I were in our courtship days. We did try to make our courtship interesting and memorable in many ways, but a practice that characterized the times we spent together was the vision we shared about how we wanted different aspects of our lives to be. One area we talked about often and prayed about was parenting. In fact, my husband had started praying about his kids before he met me. So, for him when our babies arrived it was like he was meeting someone in person he had already met in prayer before! For me on the other hand, I started to pray intentionally during courtship for my kids. But I must say that it was not easy keeping to a daily commitment of praying in details for them.

When the children began to arrive, it increasingly became difficult to schedule prayer times specifically for them as so many other obligations seemed to interrupt. Prayer for the kids became more like sporadic actions, not a deliberate system created to consistently uphold my children in prayer. This was the situation until the Lord woke me up to the indispensable necessity of praying consistently for my children.

A wise man once said that the abuse of a thing is inevitable once the purpose of that thing is not known. There are roles and responsibilities that God has placed on mothers to fulfill. Succeeding at your role of being a mother will require you to thoroughly understand what the role is and how important it is especially as it relates to God's divine plan.

"But we were gentle among you, just as a nursing mother cherishes her own children." 1 Thessalonians 2:7

"My son, hear the instruction of your father, And do not forsake the law of your mother; For they will be a graceful ornament on your head, And chains about your neck." Proverbs 1:8

"Ahaziah the son of Ahab became king over Israel in Samaria in the seventeenth year of Jehoshaphat King of Judah, and reigned two years over Israel. He did evil in the sight of the Lord, and walked in the way of his father and in the way of his mother and in the way of Jeroboam the son of Nebat, who had made Israel sin; for he served Baal and worshiped him, and provoked the Lord God of Israel to anger, according to all that his father had done." 1Kings 22:51-53

These scriptures show that we as mothers have the important roles of nurturing, teaching, and training to play in our children's lives. We could either model the wrong or the right things, and what we do ultimately determines the direction their lives go and the outcome of their lives.

A mother's role is not just to birth her babies into physical existence, she is also responsible for birthing her babies through prayer into their divine destinies. She births them physically by pushing with the grace and strength God gives her in the delivery room, but she births their destinies by the P.U.S.H (pray until something happens) she gives in the war room!

Mothers have two birthing responsibilities in the life of a child. The first one prepares you for the second one. Every mother desires to see her children become successful and most importantly to become all that God has purposed for them. There is no doubt that you want the best for your children. You also understand the power of praying for your child. That may be why you picked this book. Chances are that you are presently like me who once also had to go through the phase of motherhood as a mum to toddlers and Pre-scholars, or you have kids who are in elementary school and who are becoming adolescents, or you are at the stage I am at present, which is being a mum to teenagers and tweenies. At whichever stage you are, motherhood can be daunting and overwhelming and would necessitate the wisdom in setting priorities that would be in the best interest of your children. Knowing what is most important and executing it on time will have the spiral effect of creating ease in other aspects of your roles as a mother.

As a mother, there is no better legacy you can give your children than that of the power and effect of your prayers in their lives. In today's world which is principally driven by perception, a lot of women are focused on the glamour and the glitz, what we call 'Efizi' when making choices concerning their children. They give priority to and are overly more concerned about the schools their kids attend, the clothes they wear, holiday spots they visit, and all that. While this is important, you'll be mistaken if you think that these physical and fleeting provisions surpass investing spiritual fuel into the destinies of your children. You may not be able to go everywhere with your kids, but your prayers accompany them everywhere they go. Your prayers mold and shape them in numerous ways. It activates heaven's resources on their behalf. It protects them and delivers them from evil. It helps them through their struggles and catalyzes their overall well-being and significance here on earth. Throughout scriptures, mothers have been the significant factors who receive divine intentions from God about their children. I believe these are occurrences that point to the valuable role a mother is expected to play in seeing that their children bear the fruits of their divine ordination and consecration.

You are a mother on a mission. You are not just meant to have babies and do every other thing nicely except, labor and travail for their souls in prayer. Mum, it is time to put on your full armor and take the posture of war and fight for your seed to manifest his or her full glory. Luke 1:42 is the portrait of a woman on a mission.

"And she spoke out with a loud voice, and said. Blessed are you among women and blessed is the fruit of your womb." Luke 1:42

Mum, you are blessed, and that means your seed is blessed. A lion can only give birth to a lion. Going on our knees in continual supplication for our seed will make this scripture become reality in our lives.

I have been a mother now for over two decades. It has been a journey of many parts. There were times when I was practically clueless on what to do, whether it was preparing for the arrival of my child, choosing the right name, managing a child that was struggling with a bad habit or behavioral trait, or one with academic challenges, or even a baby who would not eat or is always cranky. At such times, I have looked to God for wisdom, sought the help of older mums, or just read up some information that helped.

Parenting can be painfully difficult. I can tell you

that, it is sure easier to write about parenting than being a parent. I remember when my second child was about six months old and I had traveled with her to a particular city which was three and a half-hour drive from the city I lived in then. We had just spent a few days there when she took ill. I had thought it was a mere fever, but with days going by, the fever graduated into other symptoms and it got critical. She was no longer keeping any food in her system. Even the drugs she took passed out immediately after I administered them. I had a few family members with me, but I felt alone. As a Christian, my first recluse was God. This scripture came to mind.

"And in the thirty ninth year of his reign, Asa became diseased in his feet and his malady was severe; yet in his disease he did not seek the Lord, but the physicians." 2 Chronicles 16:12

I did not want to be like Asa. My husband and I believe in the miracle healing power of God. I prayed fervently for my girl, but this was one situation that God seemed not to come fast enough. My husband was always on the phone declaring God's word over his daughter. I remember one night after we had been on admission in three hospitals and her situation wasn't improving, I gave up the fight. Yes. Mothers can get overwhelmed and reach that breaking point where you seem hopeless. I came to my wit's end. I was tired from sleepless nights, and watching the distress of a little innocent soul. That was where I got to. And I remember saying to myself, Father I'm not doing this again and I won't be surprise if I wake up and she is gone. I'm over with this. I took a supposedly last look at my daughter laying sick and weak by my side and in my "give-up state," I silently said good-bye and slept off like a baby.

Expecting to see a dead child, I woke up the next morning and here was my daughter, she was very much awake and alive. Sometimes we pray and get instant answers but at other times our miracles do not come immediately but with time. However, from the moment we pray, God hears and He answers us with a Yes.

"For all the promises of God in Him are yes and in him Amen, to the glory of God through us." 2 Corinthians 1:20

I knew from that moment that God in His mercy had ignored the foolish utterances I made in my moment of weakness and answered my prayer and that of everyone praying to restore my daughter's health. This was the beginning of her healing without one more drug! Though I had become weak and tired because of the sleepless nights of watching over her, I had started out praying and believing for my daughter's healing, her father was standing in faith, family members were supportive. God responded to our prayer and faith.

Prayer is a spiritual weapon that does not fail.

This book is to point young mothers and aspiring mums to the one most important responsibility they have to their children. It is so much power that has already been handed down to us mothers by the real owner of these children. We are just caretakers and directors and our homes are the boot-camps and training grounds where these lives must be molded and equipped for divine destiny.

The information here is to inspire and guide you to focus on a continuous and persistent prayer investment into your children. A whole chapter is dedicated to prayers you can offer for your children. The scriptures that inspired each prayer are provided to enable you to meditate, allow the Holy Spirit to expand it in your mind, and at the same time fit it to your unique situation. Also, there are some confessions to make for you and your children.

This book will be helpful to aspiring mothers as well. It is never too early to start praying for your children.

There are promises in the scriptures that gives us the assurance that our prayers will be heard and answered.

I desire to inspire and challenge every woman who picks this book to pay the prayer price for their children and for the generations unborn. I pray that a burden to become your children's intercessor will grab a hold of you and propel you in the direction of fulfilling this great mandate.

CATALYZE

CHAPTER ONE

WHAT ABOUT PRAYER?

"Then you will call on me and go and pray to me, and I will listen to you." Jeremiah 29:12

"Call to me, and I will answer you, and show you great and mighty things which you do not know." Jeremiah 33:3

Prayer is a spiritual conversation or communication between man and God. It is an act of supplication or intercession directed toward a deity (God). It is important that we clearly comprehend the character and nature of prayer in order to pray better.

We need to understand that in prayer we should not only talk to God but listen to Him. It is like a child having a conversation with his father, what usually occurs is mutual communication. We see this kind of dialogue between God and Abraham as touching his intention to destroy Sodom in Genesis 18. There are many promises in God's word to encourage us to pray.

"Ask, and it will be given to you; seek, and you will find; knock and it will be opened to you." **Matthew 7:7**

We will always short change ourselves when we make prayer just an exercise where you only talk to God, but we fail to listen to Him.

Prayer is more than a conversation, but it is also a time of fellowship and intimacy with God, where His divinity envelops our humanity and this result in multiplied strength, rare wisdom, and unexplained peace and joy.

"...But those who wait on the Lord shall renew their strength; They shall mount up with wings like eagles; They shall run and not be weary, they shall walk and not faint." Isaiah 40:31

The scripture also assures us that when we pray God hears and answers us.

"Now this is the confidence that we have in him, that if we ask anything according to his will, he hears us. And if we know that he hears us, whatever we ask, we know that we have the petitions that we have asked of him" 1 John 5:14-15

When you receive Christ into your heart, you become

a child of God and he becomes your father. This new relationship gives you the privilege of talking to him in prayer at any time about anything, just the same way that you would walk into your earthly father's room at any time to discuss anything without reservation or restriction.

"Therefore, brethren, having boldness to enter the Holiest by the blood of Jesus, by a new and living way which he consecrated for us through the veil, that is, his flesh." Hebrews 10:19

"Let us therefore come boldly to the throne of grace, that we may obtain mercy and find grace to help in time of need." Hebrews 4:16

"Praying always with all prayer and supplication in the spirit, being watchful to this end with all perseverance and supplication for all the saints." Ephesians 6:18

We may ask, why should I pray? Great! We pray because we are commanded to pray. So many times in scripture we read that we should be in continual prayer.

"Pray without ceasing." 1 Thessalonians 5:17-18

"Be anxious for nothing, but in everything by

prayer and supplication, with thanksgiving, let your request be made known to God and the peace of God which surpasses all understanding, will guard your hearts and minds through Christ Jesus." Philippians 4:6-7

"And he spake a parable unto them to this end, that men ought always to pray and not lose heart" Luke 18:1

Through our prayers, we can make our request known to God. God is eager to grant us our request especially when it aligns with his will.

"Now this is the confidence that we have in him, that, if we ask anything according to his will, he hears us: And if we know that he hears us, whatever we ask, we know that we have the petitions that we have asked of him." 1 John5:14-15

Very importantly also, prayer enables us to discern God's will. We can begin to understand and gain clarity of purpose when we commune and stay in tune with God in the place of prayer. God wants to guide us. He does not expect us to go through life in a limbo, like one with a blindfold who is constantly stumbling and sustaining terrible injuries. "Call to me, and I will answer you, and show you great and mighty things, which you do not know." Jeremiah 33;3

As we constantly pray, our faith in a dependable and reliable father in heaven grows. Prayer is the arena where our faith is always boosted. "But you, beloved, building yourselves up on your most holy faith, praying in the Holy Spirit." Jude 20

Prayer helps us overcome the temptations of the devil. The devil always wants to use our weaknesses as strongholds against us, but with prayer, we are alert and vigilant to avoid his schemes. Jesus asked his disciples to be delivered from evil and temptation. **"....and do not lead us into temptation, but deliver us from the evil one." Luke 11:4.**

Prayer helps us face and overcome the struggles and challenges of life and it strengthens us daily. **"Be anxious for nothing , but in everything by prayer and supplication, with thanksgiving, let your request be made known to God, which surpasses all understanding, will guard your hearts and minds through Christ." Philippians 4:6**

Prayer changes us. Imagine that you spend a lot of time cooking with firewood in an enclosed local African kitchen, your clothes and body would have absorbed the smoke from the firewood and you start to smell of smoke. In the same way, when we spend time with God we absorb his traits and begin to look more like Him. It is in prayer that God molds our character and refines us for life. The more we spend time with Him, the more we become like Him. **"But we all, with unveiled face, beholding as in a mirror the glory of the Lord, are being transformed into the same image from glory to glory, just as by the Spirit of the Lord."   2 Corinthians 3:18**

Through prayer we provide God's protective cover over our loved ones. Prayer also bring breakthroughs to us when we don't know what else to do, where else to go, how else to do. When we are stuck, overwhelmed, threatened by just anything, clueless, or seem to have exhausted all avenues, we can leverage our prayers to receive a heavenly intervention. Sometimes we need to get away, retreat, fast, and pray to get a word or direction from God. **"Likewise the Spirit also helps in our weaknesses; For we do not know what we should pray for as we ought , but the Spirit Himself makes intercession for us with groanings which cannot be uttered." Romans 8:26**

You might think: Oh! But anybody can pray for my children, their daddy, aunties, uncles, grandmas and grandpas, pastors, and other persons. I don't need to bury myself in prayer for them. I am so busy trying to get them going in other areas. Yes, this is quite true as anyone can pray for your child. But you need to understand that rarely will somebody carry a burden for your child like you would the child directly entrusted to you.

Realize that I didn't say the child you gave birth to. You don't have to be the biological mother of a child before you can play a mother's role in that child's life. ***People are more concerned about their headaches than they are about your cancer.*** In other words, human nature is selfish, moreover, everyone is dealing with his or her issues. Whether you bore or adopted this child, as long as this child has been entrusted to your care, your mother's instinct should make you willing to go down for this child. A mother's instinct is what separates the kind of love you have for your child from the love others have for them.

Also, God has purposed the mother (biological or otherwise) of a child to be the perfect candidate who can effectively transform and impact their child's life. Mum, you are the one meant to pray for your children, because you spend more time with them and therefore know them more deeply than any other person.

Throughout scripture, we see that most of the time the mother was the one who received a prophetic word about the child. Instances of these are Mary, concerning Jesus, and Hannah, concerning Samuel. This just shows that God would usually hand over to the mother the prophetic blueprint for the child so that she can "war a good warfare" with those prophecies.

THE CHALLENGE

Parenting comes with numerous challenges. Successful parenting borders primarily on love, wisdom, and discipline. God will never give you an assignment without adequately empowering you to succeed in it.

God never sets us up for failure.

No matter how difficult and challenging the situations you may have had or that you are presently experiencing in your parenting journey, it does not make you a failure. God rather allows us to experience these difficult seasons because they wake us up to embrace growth and transformation. Always remember that God has a plan.

"My brethren, count it all joy when you fall into various trials, knowing that the testing of your faith produces patience. But let patience have its perfect work, that you may be perfect and

complete, lacking nothing." James 1:2-3

None of us become experts at parenting from the beginning, but as we yield daily to God's grace upon us, his wisdom in our hearts and the support we get from family and friends we become better at the role.

The woman is the heart of the home. Her beat and rhythm determines to a great measure the atmosphere and dynamics of the family.

Being a woman, a mother can wear many hats which can be quite demanding and difficult when not properly managed. Often a mum is a wife at home, a staff or an executive at work, an entrepreneur or business owner outside her home, a Pastor, minister, or worker in the church, and many more roles that call for her special wiring and gender. She has her hands full with taking care of the kids, fixing the meals, working on her business or career and having to meet deadlines, helping the kids with homework and she has to be there for her children's school events, the list is endless.

With a full schedule, most times a mother might not have as much time for prayer as she should. By this, I mean a special time dedicated to praying for her children alone, not the family devotional time in the mornings, which are usually short. I can fully relate to this, because having raised children who are now teenagers with many other children growing up in my home at the same time, and I being quite a younger woman at the time who was learning the ropes of being a Pastor's wife, I was mum to my young children, a worker in the church, women ministry leader, business owner, and student, it was like living the lives of ten people at the same time.

With all these going on, it becomes difficult for some women to have adequate time dedicated to supplicating for their children. Most nights, after a full day I get so exhausted that all I want to do is sleep. What happens here is that, praying for your children can become a circumstantial response rather than a planned and deliberate practice, it becomes an emergency fix, a riotous remedy rather than a systematic, intentional time of communication with the Father. I had to learn not to wait for a crisis before I pray for my children. I am talking about building a prayer bank you can always draw upon.

Eventually, I figured out that though I had a lot on my plate and I was busy with other things, I needed to be intentional by simply drawing up a schedule inclusive of prayer time for my kids during my energy hours. When you begin to understand the importance and value of deliberately praying for your children, then you will rate it as a priority practice on your to-do-list.

Until a mum understands the rewards of praying for her child, she may not be willing to stake her life for it. There is awesome power released to shape and sharpen their destiny when you deliberately pray for your children. Amidst prayers, sometimes our children still derail from the right path, but the situation is usually curtailed and controlled because we have been praying. When a mother begins to pray for her child early, what she is doing in essence is creating a reservoir and wealth of help, interventions, and miracles that attends to the child as he or she journeys through life.

While the challenges of parenting are real, the results of being intentional and pushing past the difficulties are quite rewarding. Some glaring struggles a mother would experience are:

INADEQUATE TIME

While everyone is blessed with 24 hours daily and it seems like much time, for a mum it may be quite limited. She has to juggle all the roles she plays, and she might still find it hard to fix all the important things such as prayer time into her schedule. But I believe that if 24 hours wasn't adequate for a successful destiny, God would have given us more.

Nobody has time to pray until they create time to pray.

Until you make time to pray for your children, you will seldom have the time for it. Being that praying is a somewhat difficult task, we tend to push it to the last thing we want to do and we end up not doing it because we have no energy left. You need to dedicate more time outside your morning quiet-time to pray for your children.

The kind of prayer I recommend here the most is praying in the Spirit. How to handle this will be to do the praying while involved in tasks that concern your kids. I call it praying on the move. While bathing them, fixing their meals, driving them to school or to an event, pray for them and pray with them. Talk to God constantly about them.

Iniobong, who has been married for over two decades and a mother of four says, *"As a wife, mother and career woman, I wear many hats and this has informed a prayer schedule that works for me. I pray every morning before going to work and this is what I have maintained, however, I have made it one of my goals this year to set aside a day every month to fast and pray for my children".*

Elizabeth Amuta, a busy academic, a wife for over four decades and mother of five adult children however, says *"Praying for my children is a normal flow for me as I pray every day. My prayers in the morning are always with my husband and we pray for them together and at any other times during the day or night. It has also always been our family tradition to fast and pray together every Friday for the family. Fasting and vigils often go with other special times of dedicated prayers as needs arise. Though I sometimes felt I did not have enough time to pray."* Don't most mothers feel this same way?

"Look carefully then how you walk! Live purposefully and worthily and accurately, not as the unwise and witless, but as wise (sensible, intelligent people) Making the very most of the time, buying up each opportunity, because the days are evil." Ephesians 5:15-16(Amplified)

From this scripture, a key word we should consider is being purposeful. Praying for the kids should be deliberate, prioritized and valued, not trivialized. We see that this is our weaponry against the enemy. It is unwise and insensible to neglect this assignment, and give excuses of never having the time. So if you struggle with inadequate time, get intentional and schedule what works for you, then commit to it. When we use our time well, we are transacting profitably for the kingdom, but when we waste time on what is useless, we are giving the enemy room.

MISPLACED PRIORITY

Some mothers mistakenly esteem the need to provide for their kid's material, physical, emotional, intellectual, and social needs above the spiritual. The thinking that what your kid need the most are good clothes, shoes, food, shelter, education, and social skills, at the expense of a strong and consistent spiritual input. This is misleading. Don't get me wrong, while they need all of these areas fixed, the balance is for us to as well, invest prayer and spiritual grooming into their lives. You have the opportunity to give them a gift beyond comparison by taking their current and future needs to God. Teaching them how to pray gives them an indispensable spiritual skill they can always fall back on when on their own as they face the challenges of life. Your faithful prayer input into the lives of your children can deliver to them in the future what money and material things will not and cannot deliver.

"The prayer of a righteous person has great power as it is working." James 5:16 ESV.

DISCOURAGEMENT

One time, I had to seek the Lord about a struggle my child had and I prayed for a long time. You know when a prayer point keeps popping up on the prayer list all the time, the question you will ask is; "Oh God, are you there?" This was my case. I became discouraged and I was tempted to stop praying. You may find yourself where you start to doubt God's faithfulness, then make conclusions like: God is not interested in answering this particular prayer or God might be punishing one of my sins, or you utter things like "this is not working," "my child is not going to change." At this point you may begin to lose faith, but you can draw strength from this scripture:

"Be anxious for nothing, but in everything by prayer and supplication with thanksgiving let your request be made known unto God." Philippians 4:6

We need to understand that prayer is an investment, and our faith in the sacrifice Jesus made for us to receive answers to our prayers is the down payment, which is guaranteed and sealed by the name of Jesus.

We pray in the name of Jesus and His name never fails. Every request bearing that name never bounces back! Hallelujah! The cheque always clears! God can be depended on, He is not like a man that might give you a dud cheque.

Sometimes we see the answers to our prayers long after we have prayed.
At such times of waiting, we do not faint in well-doing, we keep our eyes on the promise and eventually we are witnesses of what we prayed for.

As a mum I have come to conclude that prayer is my best bet, especially knowing that all other physical remedies applied can prove abortive. What do you do with a child who never heeds to your instructions and becomes rebellious, or a child who is always sickly and in hospital, or one who is struggling academically even after putting all measures in place, or one who resorts to drugs, pornography, cultism, immorality and all other forms of vices regardless of your love, discipline, and godly training? Prayer is the way to go, where you cast your cares on God.

> ***God might not show up in your own time,***
> ***but he will ultimately show up***
> ***at the nick of time, to save your***
> ***baby from harm and destruction.***

"So don't give up and stop praying because you don't see any physical evidence that your

prayer is answered." Galatians 6:9

Remember Daniel prayed and his prayer ascended immediately to the throne of God. In fact God answered, but he did not receive the physical manifestation because Satan hindered it for 21 days. At such times you take a faith stand to quench all the fiery darts of the wicked.

Elizabeth Amuta attests that *"Praying regularly with my husband for our children has helped us a lot because details appear to be covered quite well and when we experience the unexpected, we have seen the power of continued prayer straightening things out."*

"One incidence comes to mind and that was about my second daughter's choice of subjects at 'O level'. I did not expect any problem hoping that her strongest subjects would ordinarily define whether she will be in Sciences, Commercial or Arts class. At the end of SS1 it was obvious she couldn't handle Chemistry but she was not happy because Dad, Mum, and her two older siblings were all in the Sciences. It was a serious struggle for her because she didn't want to be the odd one. An inferiority complex was going to be inevitable. I saw the need to have prayed better than I did. With more intentional prayers and counseling, she accepted her obvious God-given talent in the arts. Today she is such an excellent speaker, coach, and

development consultant. I am ever grateful for answered prayers. Hallelujah!" Praise God! Do you see the habit of continued prayer stressed here? We don't just pray once or twice, then give up just because we haven't seen the answers with the physical eyes. We see through the eyes of faith. We believe we receive. We count it done and it is settled!

LACK OF KNOWLEDGE

How do I pray? What do I pray? This can pose a challenge to some mothers.

"The labour of fools wearies them, For they do not even know how to go to the city!" Ecclesiastes 10:15

Some mothers struggle with praying for their children because they do not know how to.

> *Becoming a praying mother does not occur by taking Master classes, rather we all learn to pray by praying.*

Just like you learn patience by being patient, so also you learn to pray by showing up to pray. As you study the Word of God on prayer and exercise yourself in the place of prayer you become good at it and comfortable in it.

***The art of Prayer is not exclusively
for some people who term themselves
'prayer warriors', but for all Believers
who will give themselves to praying.***

In Christ, we all have equal access to the presence of God, as well as a right to all the covenant provisions. This is so good. You don't have to beg or plead or wait for permission to come. You can grace His presence confidently and comfortably at anytime and anywhere you choose. The blood has created access for you and I. Through the blood we enter blameless, guiltless and shameless.

"Let us therefore come boldly to the throne of grace, that we may obtain mercy, and find grace to help in time of need." Hebrews 4:16

"Therefore, brethren, having boldness to enter the Holiest by the blood of Jesus, by the new and living way which he consecrated for us through the veil, that is , His flesh." Hebrews 10:19-20

All you need to do is simply initiate a conversation with your heavenly Father as you would with an earthly father without hesitation or prejudice and you are guaranteed always to have His attention, audience and response. There are several promises God has given to us for our children, all we need to do is take those same scriptures back to Him as a reminder to fulfill them in their lives. There are no better prayer points than affirming the promises in scriptures concerning our little ones.

Another good way to raise prayer points for your kids is to look at what is presently going on in their lives which, most likely needs divine intervention; your exasperation and expectation about them can be converted to a prayer request. How about the prophecies you have received at various times concerning them? You can war good warfare in the place of prayer with those good words.

Elizabeth Amuta shares further on how she prays for her children. She says, *"I raise prayers to cover the areas of obedience and love for God; seeking God with all their hearts; the quest for things of eternal value; knowing their callings and gifts and serving God faithfully. I also pray that they make the right choices in small or big matters; for people in their lives [spouses, children, friends, mentors, pastors, in-laws, colleagues, and so on]. I pray for them to stand and overcome in trials and temptations, to love and greatly impact their world for Christ, to enjoy all-round prosperity, provisions, preservation, protection wherever and whenever in life; to be distinguished in excellence; for wisdom, knowledge, and understanding, discernment, direction, and self-control.*

Other prayers I raise for my children are for the fullness of the fruit of the Holy Spirit; that they and all the generations after them will enjoy good long lives; never to fear, get discouraged or frustrated; to enjoy the overcomer's life and to make heaven. I use various relevant scriptures sometimes from Genesis, Psalms, Proverbs, and through the New Testament to purposefully pray the word or I pray freely as led by the Holy Spirit."

Once you can use the scripture as a guide, you will never miss it. Commit your prayer time to the Holy Spirit and he will teach you and help you. He is a reliable helper.

LAZINESS AND PROCRASTINATION

I had mentioned earlier that praying is not an easy task and requires the discipline to be faithful and consistent. While prayer is a purely spiritual exercise that the Holy Spirit enables and assists us to do, we are the ones expected to initiate the process.

The Holy Spirit is a helper, not a doer

Being lazy about praying and always deferring prayer time can become a huge challenge. Sometimes you are not very busy, but then you may not even be willing to take advantage of any window of time you have to pray. The thinking is that you can always pray tomorrow; tomorrow comes and it's still not a better time, so you defer still to another 'tomorrow'. When you add up all the many 'tomorrows' you will then realize that it has become years of not making adequate prayer investments into the lives of your children. Time breezes by, then you realize afterwards that you wasted your most valuable years not doing the right thing, and now the children are grown up. May this not be your story!

We can learn discipline and grit from the ant.

"Go to the ant, you sluggard! Consider her ways and be wise, Which, having no captain,overseer,or ruler, provides her supplies in the summer, and gathers her food in the harvest. How long will you slumber, O sluggard? When will you rise from your sleep?" Proverbs 6:6-8

Laziness is a habit. A lazy person is full of excuses of why they can't get the work done. God has given the recreated human spirit the ability to make the body do all things. In 2 Tim 1:7Amp, it is called the spirit of self-control and discipline. Smith Wigglesworth said his body, feelings or emotions don't tell him what to do or feel, rather he (referring to his inner man) tells his body how to feel and what to do. This is what living from the inside out means. This is how we thrive as Christians.

"The ants are a people not strong, yet they prepare their food in the summer" Proverbs 30:25

WEARINESS

This may sound similar to inadequate time, but what I mean here is that mothers set themselves up to get exhausted and so become weary – having no strength to pray.

"She rises while it is yet night and gets spiritual food for her household and assigns her maids their task." Proverbs 31:15 (Amplified)

Anybody will be unable to pray when they are tired and fagged out. A mum should deploy wisdom to conserve energy to pray. When you overwork yourself with other activities, you are not left with any more energy to meet up with some other crucial obligations. It's just like a married woman who works tirelessly during the day and at night she can't give herself to her husband in bed. Though all the work she did during the day is legitimate, she did not consider a very important role she could have conserved energy for in preparation for delivering what only she can give her husband.

> *A mother on a mission will delegate*
> *what is delegate-able*
> *So that she can do what cannot be delegated.*

The weariness and heart-ache the child whose life does not turn out well can bring to you parents is too great for you to consider succumbing to the foolishness of neglecting to pray for your child. Now you may say I can delegate others to pray for my kids. While this may be true, it is not rocket science that since prayer is relationship-based, making it mechanical may not bring much results.

> *No one can pray for your kids better*
> *than you can do. The empathy and*
> *passion you bring into the place*
> *of prayer Is irreplaceable.*

Dear mum, you are a mother on a mission!

When you check every woman in the Bible beginning with Mother Eve you would see that the physical birthing of her children was just the first phase of her assignment. She was meant to ensure that they were adequately nurtured and groomed to fulfill their divine destinies. This is what I call the second birthing! And I discovered that this second birthing is catalyzed by a spiritual push, unlike the first one which requires a physical push. Mum if you can push the first time at the instructions of the midwife to birth your baby, you can better push the second time as a mandate from God to birth their destinies here on earth. *To P.U.S.H is to pray until something happens!* That is, we start to pray and do not stop until we see the result of our prayers in our children. Oh, what a noble but herculean task! But you have been given grace.

"...for as soon as Zion travailed, she brought forth her children." Isaiah 66:8 (KJV)

At times I do not feel like I have prayed enough for my kids, and I cannot say that I have been the perfect praying mum, but I have known seasons when I prayed earnestly and received answers.

Like I earlier stated, the instruction to write this book came six months after I started a prayer group for mothers. The vision for creating a platform for mothers to get the support and accountability to pray for their kids dropped in my heart one beautiful afternoon when I was in a conversation with a dear spiritual daughter. We talked about how fast our kids were growing and spoke about how soon we would have to attend each other's children's weddings which will require buying *asoebi* (a dress code). But as we laughed and got excited at this, some thoughts filled my heart – the thought of seeing our children reflecting the prayers we have prayed for them, the thought of their future being ironed out with little or no casualty situations, like finding and marrying their man of God or woman of God, gaining quick employment, serving the Lord fervently with their families, running successful businesses, living in good health, having kids when they should have, doing well financially and on and on. At that moment it dawned on me that it is only when mothers pay the prayer price that they would be guaranteed the more genuine and authentic joy and a peace of mind. Only prayer gives you cock-sure assurance when the kids grow up and leave the house that all will go well. This is better than just being merely fascinated with the fact that they are grown and are leaving house.

So the question to every mother is, "Who is leaving your home? Is he or she a success going to happen or a failure going to happen?" The onus is on you. The future we talked about is already here. It surprised me how my once cute little princesses are now grown and being admired by the opposite sex.

Since that conversation took place, a burden which I believe came from God dropped in my heart. *I saw a community of mothers who are conscious and intentional about the mandate of a second birthing process that requires the same if not a stronger passion and determination to accomplish for the love of the young ones they bear. I saw a support system that could help the next young mother navigate her journey of birthing; I saw the middle-aged mother whose strength was failing receiving just the encouragement needed to keep going."*

In my struggles as a young mother, I had at times desired to have another mother partner with me in prayer over my children, and I am convinced this is a dire need for so many other mothers as well. I envisaged that two or three women coming together in prayer would help mothers pray better, and encouraged them to share their peculiar prayer needs as well as celebrate their victories together.

Wow! As I meditated deeper on the need for mothers to pray for their kids I was not thinking about myself alone, but my heart went out to all mothers and aspiring mothers. I am convinced that prayer is the best investment we can make into the lives of our children.

CHAPTER THREE

THE REWARD

Our prayers do not die. They are ever alive before God! Yes, I am excited about this. The reward of praying for your children has a dual effect: it positively impacts the child and it impacts the mother as well. The value of prayer is felt by the person who prays and the one who is being prayed for.

What is one's life without prayer? Man is reward-driven. When you know the benefit and value you get from an investment that is sold to you, it becomes a motivation to consider buying into it. Here I intend to share with you the possible gains you would get when you decide to commit to investing regular, word-based prayer into your children.

YOU ENJOY THE REWARD OF OBEDIENCE

Scriptures command that we should pray. Through prayer, we commune with God on a daily based.

"For this is the love of God, that we keep his commandments: and his commandments are not BURDENSOME." 1 John 5:3. God's instructions carry with them the grace for us to obey. He won't give us a load we can't carry. Even His burdens are light. God rewards the obedient person with goodness and prosperity. From the scriptures, Jesus, teaching his disciples stated that **"men always ought to pray and not lose heart" (Luke 18:1).** He goes further to show how prayer should be offered. This prayer format is the template delivered to us by the Lord himself.

Taking a careful look at the *Lord's Prayer* in **Luke 11:2-4,** we see the elements of prayer covering different areas of needs. We see that prayer begins with worship to the Father as a crucial protocol to his presence, then we see the need to address the will of God in our prayer first before focusing on our personal needs. Jesus said **'pray thy kingdom come here on earth as it is in heaven'.** Jesus did not just command us to pray but modeled a lifestyle of prayer to emphasize the importance of praying. If Jesus who was anointed without measure needed to pray, then we need it much more.

"And when he had sent them away, he departed to the mountain to pray." Mark 6:46

"Take heed, watch and pray; for you do not know when the time is." Mark 13:33

"Pray without ceasing" 1 Thessalonians 5:17

When you develop a habit of praying and interceding for your children, great chances are that your children will turn out to be prayerful too. Your children will normally model after you. Much more effective than a systematic regular sermon on prayer is the example of a praying mum.

DEPENDENCE ON GOD

Parenting being a task that requires wisdom, understanding, intuition, and grace cannot be effective without the help of God. Praying will grant you abundant grace on your parenting journey. It is the means by which you humble yourself before God to obtain His much needed help.

"God resists the proud, but gives grace to the humble." 1 Peter 5:5

It takes humility to cast all the cares and anxiety you have about your children on God in prayer and to refuse to worry. To pray for your child is admittance that there is a higher wisdom, power, and authority beside you, which can help to navigate their lives through any struggle, pressure, or sin. So with prayer, you can access the wealth of heaven's resources to improve your parenting. You can also stand in the stead of God as you pray for your children to release heaven's help, provisions, and interventions into their lives.

Like Hannah in the bible, many women seem to have all going for them, but an aspect of their lives depicts barrenness. I think sometimes God allows that one gap or dent in our lives so that we can remain dependent on Him. It is so easy to forget God. when all is well! While I don't believe God afflicts us with pain to enslave us, I strongly believe He allows us to go through some kind of difficult experience so that we can acknowledge His omnipotence, strengthen our dependence on Him, and to grow our faith

PROTECTION FROM SATANIC ATTACK

"Be sober, be vigilant, because your adversary the devil walks about like a roaring lion seeking whom he may devour. Resist him, steadfast in the faith, knowing that the same sufferings are experienced by your brotherhood in the world." 1Peter5:8

We see here that right after casting our cares on God, we should be careful to watch our doors against Satan's attacks, because he is always lurking around to inflict and afflict us if permitted. Constantly praying for your children is how you build a hedge of protection around them against the devil's wiles. Your prayer is the lock that shuts the enemy out of their lives. Hallelujah!

Rose shares a beautiful testimony of how God delivered her son from the satanic claws of molesters because she dared to pray. She says: *"one of those times that I went into prayer for them, I had a strong urge to pray for my first son in the 2017-2018 academic session. Initially, I could not get clarity so when the urge came, I would just pray in the language of the Spirit. Then one day, I just knew that it was time to change his school, but his dad would not hear of it. I called my son and asked if he wanted to go back where he was and he said, "No". I begged his dad, but he said I had not given him reasons enough, so he would not change his school. Reluctantly my son resumed. He kept having serious health challenges and his grades kept dropping. I became more concerned and intensified my prayers. I would call to ask questions, but I couldn't get any answers. He completely shut me out. So on one of his visiting days, the Lord suddenly opened my eyes and I saw that he was lost in the desert wandering afar; I called him repeatedly but there was no response. Just like it started, the vision disappeared. So when they came home for the holidays I was led to teach on sexual sins, what the Bible says and the consequences of going to hell, and all that. We made some affirmative declarations and he went back.*

On the 29th of May 2018. It was a Tuesday and a public holiday too. I woke up with strong feelings to pray for him. I prayed and prayed yet the burden didn't lift. So I went to Church for Tuesday prayers. As we were praying, a word of knowledge came about a woman's son who has been under an attack but that today God has given him deliverance and he will be removed from that situation. I keyed in and immediately found peace. That evening we got a call to be in their school the next day.

To cut a long story short, my son was being molested by some male students in the school and they had sworn him to secrecy, to avoid them he had been skipping meals and sleeping in the bush which resulted in his poor health and academic challenges. He finally had had enough of that and on his own, confessed it all to the Head Boy that same Tuesday that I was praying for him. As a result, they were able to round up all those involved. He was expelled for not telling the school when it started. But for me, it worked out for his good because he left the school and found Christ and healing. That's what prayer can do. My failure here was that I wasn't patient enough to listen. I should have insisted on his transfer that first time, and perhaps all of these would not have happened. I blamed myself for many months before getting my own healing too".

The fervent prayers of a mother work effectually. I feel from my experience that it is good for any young lady of marriageable age hoping to be a mum someday to start praying for her future children the same way she prays for her future husband. For those who did not start such prayers early, they should start praying for their kids from the very day they get married until they draw their last breath. The moment you are aware, start! The best time is NOW!!

It would interest you to know that the devil is not your friend. Your faith as a Christian is offensive to him and he would do anything to destroy you.

One of the ways the enemy likes to attack us is through attacking our loved ones, especially our children, and this is because of what they represent in our lives. Your children are your seed bearers. They carry within them your investments; they carry your legacy. They perpetuate your work and extend your frontiers. They are your strength and pride in old age. They soothe your soul and make you happy even when life is difficult. **"Behold, children are a**

heritage from the Lord, the fruit of the womb is a reward." Psalms 127:3

As Christians, our arsenal does not consist of physical weapons, but we have some proven spiritual weapons given us to enable us stand against the enemy's attacks. It is in the place of prayer that we deploy these spiritual weapons of destruction to overcome principalities, powers, rulers of the darkness of this world and spiritual wickedness in high places.

"Finally, my brethren, be strong in the Lord and in the power of his might. Put on the whole armor of God, that ye may be able to stand against the wiles of the devil. For we wrestle not against flesh and blood, but against principalities, against powers, against the rulers of the darkness of this world, against spiritual wickedness in high places. Therefore take up the whole armor of God, that you may be able to withstand in the evil day, and having done all, to stand. Stand therefore, having girded your waist with truth, and having put on the breastplate of righteousness....And take the helmet of salvation, and the sword of the Spirit, which is the word of God: praying always with all prayer and supplication in the spirit, being watchful to the end with all

perseverance and supplication for all the saints" Ephesians 6:10-18

Mums, your prayers can do much more than your fears, your agitations, exasperations, and tears; it can do more than your words of doubt and unbelief. Yes, I remember nursing fears about my kids at a time, until God had to reassure me while I was several miles away from home, at a time my mind wasn't even dwelling on that concern. God knows and feels our heart's concerns. The devil doesn't own these children and so he shouldn't exert any control over them. He shouldn't run their lives. We must arise as mothers on a mission and run our own show!

The devil can only step in if we fail to stop him!

The best time to prepare for war is when there is peace. That's why the advocacy for a commitment to regular prayer? It's because our prayers build-up to create results. It is like storing water in a reservoir where you can draw from in the day of need. When a need arises will God find a bank of prayer which He can draw upon to respond to you? I bet you on this, on the day when the enemy shows up you may not be present with your children, or maybe your emotions will get the better of you, and you may not be able to respond correctly. It is at such times you get to see the value of a full 'prayer bank' or reservoir from which God can draw from to respond to you without any fresh prayers offered.

Recently, my girls shared with me about a parallel similar experience they had at different times within a space of two months. They had near car hits. They attested that they couldn't explain how they were able to stop or hesitate to go one step further just when they did. Had they not, they would have been hit by those cars. The devil is a bastard o! I quickly attributed the foiling of car accidents to angelic activities based on the prayers we had been praying, and I gave thanks to God for His deliverance.

I shared with us earlier, about when my second baby was sick unto death. I became weak and tired after my husband and I had been praying and standing in faith for over three weeks for her healing, and nothing had changed. My husband kept faith even when I seemed to lose hope, then the answer manifested. Prayer is our Joker! I pray for you reading this now that you will not be weary or faint in well-doing, rather the Lord will give you the grace to stay steadfast in the place of prayer in Jesus' name!

GUARANTEED TO DISCOVER AND FULFILL PURPOSE

If our children would live out the full purpose of God for their lives, we need to stand in the gap for them and pray it through. Anna dedicated herself to this noble cause which I believe is the mandate upon every woman. She committed to staying in the temple continually, interceding that the prophecy of the messiah should be fulfilled. She yielded to God and was dedicated and committed to that cause. We could mistakenly think that because there was an express word about the coming of the Messiah, there wasn't any need to pray for its manifestation. But no, not just Anna prayed, but Simeon also did. Prayer releases the power of God into the physical realm to make things happen. For the conception and birth of the Messiah to happen smoothly, the grace and anointing to intercede had to come upon Anna.

Throughout scriptures, God would often reveal the prophetic destiny of children to their mothers. What God was doing in essence is giving them the prayer points or a clear direction for intercession. While we shouldn't try to navigate into what God has revealed concerning our kids through scheming and manipulation like Rebekah did, the way to do it is to pray about it. I do not doubt that Rebekah would have made life better for her two sons if she had used her prayer influence well. She could have trusted God to fulfill His counsel just by recognizing her role as an intercessor and not by interfering through manipulation. Unfortunately, sometimes mothers in an attempt to scheme their way through for their kids often shortchange themselves.

One mum, to work out what God told her about her daughter becoming a very successful and influential person, began to scheme her way to ensure she married a wealthy man. Where she was mistaken was thinking God had given her the right and role to work out her daughter's destiny by insisting on who she eventually gets married to against her daughter's wish. Her desire was based on some materialistic and shallow reasoning. The result became a troubled marriage that eventually broke the daughter's heart and marred her destiny. God intimated her about His plan for her daughter for this purpose: that she should cooperate and labor in prayer for its fulfillment. Sadly, she mishandled it. ***Though the earth belongs to God, man leased it to Satan for this season through rebellion in the Garden of Eden.*** As long as Satan has taken man's place as the god of this world, he will continue to interrupt God's plan except men pray. The arm of flesh will short-circuit you! **" whose minds the god**

of this age has blinded, who do not believe, lest the light of the gospel of the glory of Christ, who is the image of God, should shine on them."2 Corinthians 4:4

We only need to faithfully seek the Lord in prayer, interceding fervently for our children to realize God's intention for them. Imagine that your children turn out as the scripture has purposed for them? Won't that be great? There are promises over our children that should be fulfilled. God's plan for our children is always the best, better than our plans for them.

One of my husband's friends in ministry tells the story of how when he answered the call to ministry as a man in his early 20s, his mother who was an evangelical, and never spoke with tongues wept as he told her, it was finally the answer to her prayers. According to the mother's story, when she was pregnant with him, he had died in her womb. Knowing the baby in her womb was dead, she was trekking to the hospital to have the baby evacuated, when she branched into a neighboring church on the way and begged God for the life of her baby. She went on to promise God that if her baby lived, she was giving him to God to serve Him. Before she got to the hospital, her baby lived and never needed to be evacuated. She said, she had been praying over her promise to God since he was born, but had never told him because he was so stubborn and rebellious. But God went after him Himself and got him. Hallelujah! That's why she was weeping at the news of her son receiving the call to ministry.

You see, children may even resist your instructions, but they have no way of resisting your prayers.

The same is true of Kenneth Copeland, whom though his Mum and Nanny would pray over him for hours from infancy using his baby cot and pillow as a point of contact, still grew up extremely self-willed and rebellious. Even when he repented and accepted the call, these two women never gave up praying. They had made up their minds that he must do great things for God. When at the relatively early age of 70, Copeland's mum was dying, he went to God over the issue, and God told him that the woman was not sick but worn out from praying all night most of her life for her son to succeed in ministry. God told him that He won't let him fail because of the supplications of his mother, but that the woman would have to come over to heaven at that point because her body was worn out and could not carry her beyond 70. She died, but her son is still shaking the nations at almost 90 years Of age.

PRAYER BIRTHS OUR MIRACLES

Remember Hannah, she was happily married to her heartthrob. Everything seemed to be going on well for Hannah except that she was childless after several years of marriage. Hannah was a blessed woman, but with a major clause in her life. This took a toll on her relationship with her husband who was quite understanding and who truly loved her. His love couldn't stop Hannah from becoming an insecure and unfulfilled woman. **"...But to Hannah, he would give a double portion, for he loved Hannah, although the Lord had closed her womb. And her rival also provoked her severely, to make her miserable, because the Lord had closed her womb." 1 Samuel 1:5-6.**

Hannah, through intense and committed prayer was able to conceive and bear a child of her own. God answers prayers. Through committed prayers you can access the answers to your questions, solutions to your problems, and peace can be restored to your troubled soul. We see Hannah finally getting God's attention when she made a vow unto the Lord. Our needs could stretch us to breaking limits, but it is at that point of total surrender and submission to God we access his best.

"And she was in bitterness of soul, and

PRAYED to the Lord and wept in anguish. Then she made a vow and said, "O Lord of hosts, if you will indeed look on the affliction of your maidservant and remember me, and not forget Your maidservant, but will give your maidservant a male child, then I will give him to the Lord all the days of his life, and no razor shall come upon his head." And it happened, as she continued **PRAYING** before the Lord, that Eli watched her mouth. Now Hannah spoke in her heart; only her lips moved, but her voice was not heard. Therefore Eli thought she was drunk. So Eli said to her, "How long will you be drunk? Put your wine away from you!" But Hannah answered and said, "No, my Lord, I am a woman of sorrowful spirit. I have drunk neither wine nor intoxicating drink, but have **POURED OUT MY SOUL** before the Lord. Do not consider your maidservant a wicked woman, for out of the abundance of my complaint and grief I have spoken until now." Then Eli answered and said, "Go in peace, and the God of Israel grant your petition which you have asked of Him." 1 Samuel 1:10-17

Elizabeth is another woman we can learn from in the Bible. She believed in miracles. Her situation was a unique one. She was well-advanced and aged like

Sarah. Just when people thought it was over with her and that she could no longer have babies, God visited her with a son. Perhaps people have given up on you, and you have become a byword in your community, and consequently you have been labeled based on your situation. That's still fine, if you haven't given up on yourself. Prayer is the arena where faith is exercised. When we stop praying we begin to lose faith. Don't give up your faith and prayer because of a biological reality. God's power can overrule any doctor's report based on your faith in Jesus' sacrifice! Like Elizabeth, believe in miracles!

"There was in the days of Herod, the king of Judea, a certain priest named Zacharias,..His wife was of the daughters of Aaron, and her name was Elizabeth. And they were both righteous before God, walking in all the commandments and ordinances of the Lord blameless. But they had no child because Elizabeth was barren, and they were both well advanced in years.
But the angel said to him, "Do not be afraid, Zacharias, for your PRAYER is heard; and your wife Elizabeth will bear you a son, and you shall call his name" Luke 1:5, 13

PROTECTION

Jochebed was the mother of Moses. She is known for her courage and wisdom to hide her son for three months from Pharaoh's death decree. The king of Egypt had a decree out to execute all male children born to the Jews. While she was heroic for her wit and courage, it is without a doubt that she must have prayed tirelessly that her son will not be killed. ***Plans alone are not enough to protect our children, our smart plans must be backed up with prayer.*** Prayer invites the hand of God to guide, direct, and make our plans to succeed. There must have been times Jochebed was jittery and overwhelmed with fear that she may be caught, and that she would lose her son. But rather than sink deeply into fear and stay there, she called on the God of Israel to help her. I believe God heard her prayer and protected Moses all through. One of the many gains of our prayer is the limitless coverage it gives us. That's because we can't be everywhere but God is everywhere. When we call on him, he is faithful to our prayers everywhere our children go.

> ***You may not be able to go everywhere with your children, But your prayers travel with them. Your prayers can go Where your feet can't go.***

Our children face danger every day. Life is a risk. But we have a God who is our refuge and our fortress, and a very present help in trouble.

The great man of God, Lester Sumrall, was born to a praying mother. His Mum was primed to go on the missionary field when circumstances beyond her control pushed her into an early marriage with a man who won't support her missionary call, so she turned her attention to prayer. When Lester was born, he grew up to despise the religious life of his Mother, and greatly admired his irreligious father and wanted to be like him in every way. He had several close shaves with death, including getting drowned at one time and having to be pulled out of the muddy river and have all the water pumped out of his lungs before he could breathe again. One time as a teenager, he and his friends built a wooden raft and headed out to sea on a daring adventure. The wind got the better of them and they lost control, being driven far from the land until they gave up hope; but at that nick of time, a favorable wave caught them and brought them back to land. Each of these times, his mother's prayer group had been alerted by the Holy Spirit and they were praying. At age 17, he caught tuberculosis and was given up by the doctors to die. The mother refused to give him up, and prayed until he was healed. That is when he radically gave his life to Christ and went into ministry almost immediately. He ended up one of the most significant Apostolic Missionaries of the 20th century Pentecostal movement.

PRAYER SCHEDULES BREAKTHROUGHS

My husband has always been a full-time pastor. We got married while I was still undergoing the one-year national youth service which is a mandatory requirement for any college graduate in my country. So the first few years of my marriage, I was a full-time housewife still trying to figure out what I was meant to do. Income was slim. Our first baby came within our first year of marriage, so we started a family almost immediately. One would think it was just me and my husband because we were just starting a family, but our pastoral role placed a demand on us to have other people live with us. Sometimes we would have as many as ten other adults in our house when our kids were very small. Family finances were just not enough and sometimes we had to practically trust God for His next provision. But He never failed us once.

When the children were old enough to start school, we needed to start paying school fees. We prayed and trusted God and He'll always miraculously provide. Looking back over two decades later, I can say now and then whenever it was challenging to pay their fees and we prayed for a breakthrough, God answered. Prayers will schedule many breakthroughs to take care of your needs. We began to use prayer and faith to schedule increases in our standard of living rather than depending on the physical finances we could see, and it kept working. Your present financial inflow may not match the dream lifestyle you want for you and your family but you can pray yourself and your children into a breakthrough! God intervenes when we call on Him. If the widow of Zarephath had not called on God to help her, Elijah would not have shown up in her life.

HEIGHTENED SENSITIVITY
TO THE HOLY SPIRIT

Parenting is not a walk in the park neither is it for the faint-hearted. Mothers generally spend more time with their kids than fathers do. To be on top of your game in motherhood would require a great deal of wisdom. The kind of wisdom recommended here is not a general method or principle of operation that has been proven for one and can now be adopted by another. I am referring to the enlightenment you need to fit into your unique situation. As a child of God, you have the Holy Spirit living inside of you and one of His major works in you is to guide you to succeed in life. He is your inner compass. With His guidance, you will never make one mistake in parenting.

One of the ways of tuning into His frequency to be guided is by having a consistent and regular interface with Him in prayer for your children. **"However, when He, the Spirit of truth, has come, He will guide you into all truth; for He will not speak on His own authority, but whatever He hears He will speak; and He will tell you things to come." John 16:13**

Who you pray about, you know about.

One time my daughter had asked her dad and me if she could honor a friend's invitation to a birthday party. It sounded like a very basic and harmless request. But we didn't give her a response immediately. She had told us about two weeks before the time, so we had time. Then a few days to the time, she asked her dad again and her dad asked her to also get consent from me. As she began to tell me about the event, I sensed the Holy Spirit within me prompt me to ask her some questions and the more I probed, the clearer it became that what she told us was not exactly what it was. Only God who knows the details could have unraveled the plans the kids had. When she discovered I had known their plans she got her friends calling me from everywhere to convince me, but they had failed. The wiser One had revealed it to me. And thank God I was sensitive enough to hear Him and bold enough to respond to His nudging.

So as you spend time praying for your children, God begins to give you light on who they are and wisdom on how to relate with them for best results. The Bible says that the Holy Spirit is our helper and intercessor.

"And I will pray to the Father, and He will give you another Helper, that He may abide with you forever — the Spirit of truth, whom the world cannot receive, because it neither sees Him nor knows Him; but you know Him, for He dwells with you and will be in you. I will not leave you orphans; I will come to you." John 14:16-18

"But the Helper, the Holy Spirit, whom the Father will send in My name, He will teach you all things, and bring to your remembrance all things that I said to you." John 14:26

Our prayer employs the ministry of the Holy Spirit who gives us a unique blueprint to raise our children. Through prayer, God will reveal His plans to our hearts. When we become aware of this plan, it enables us to help and encourage our kids on the divine path.

At an early age, Oral Robert's mother got to know that her son had a great call of God upon him. When she told him, he rebelled against it and chose basketball instead. In fact, he so despised the idea of ministry that he left home as a teenager to pursue his basketball goals, and to get away from his mother's prayers. The day he left, his Mum prayer and begged, but he won't listen. Then she prophetically told him that if he would not come back on his own, God would bring him back in a stretcher. One day, while playing basketball, he began to puff and cough and vomit blood. It was tuberculosis. He was brought home on stretcher to die. His mum and elder sister prayed him back to health and into a mighty global healing ministry that brought millions to a saving knowledge of Christ Jesus.

HEALTHY BODIES

Sickness and disease are satanic afflictions that discomfort us and drain our family finances. When we pray for our children's health from the standpoint of the finished works of Christ, they get to enjoy good health. With an understanding of the redemptive work of Christ, we know that we do not intercede for good health, rather we just agree by faith that health and healing have been provided in the covenant and so it is available for us to enjoy. Our role as mums is to engage our faith in the promise of healing and health and to keep declaring them over our children.

Rose says, *"My children's health has improved greatly through my faith in God's healing word and prayer. The first three are asthmatic. My second son had a chronic case but it has become a thing of the past through prayers because I got some directions on what to do."* Hallelujah! You can save a lot of hospital bills just prophesying God's healing word over your children and standing in faith over their health. As a covenant daughter it is abnormal to frequent Hospitals, but only normal to know how to address the symptoms that attack your children to keep them in check. **By faith we understand that the worlds were framed by the word of God, so that the things which are seen were not made of things which are visible. Hebrews 11:3.** Speaking God's word has creative ability. By your words, you can drive sickness away from your household. With your daily prophecies, you can establish a healthy family.

ACADEMIC EXCELLENCE

Your prayers can greatly impact your children's academic performance. All areas of our life respond to prayer. The mental capacity and ability of our children can be stimulated with prayer. If you have children who are not doing so well in school, you can seek the promises of God and direct your prophesying towards their academic performance.

Iniobong testifies in this light: *"I can confidently attest to God's faithfulness in answering our prayers. When my second daughter was much younger and in elementary school, I noticed at a time she wasn't doing well in her math. I had taught them to pray and that God answers prayer. This I did by praying together with them. I made them understand how important prayer is, and it should be their first reflex action any time they were in need. We took the reoccurring poor grades in math to God in prayer and sought his intervention and he answered. She started doing well in school.*

A similar incident happened while she was in secondary school. She came to the point where she had to streamline in SS1. While she was good in all her subjects, she was skeptical about Chemistry and was misled to enroll in another subject other than Further-Mathematics. Once I discovered, I knew she was scared, so we prayed about it to clear her fears and she picked up the two subjects and did very well in both. God answers even the minutest of things. He cares about our children's academics. Once at the university, she failed two courses, which had never happened before. I prayed with her about it and we made declarations, I handed over the phone to my husband to pray with her also. Later she shared the testimony of how God helped her and she passed her courses, and this again was an answered prayer." Hallelujah!

Another mum says, *"Flourish was the best graduating student in her set and Julius is leading in his class, while Joseph is the overall best in his school as it stands. The rest are not doing badly either. They love the Lord and are striving to be the best they can be. So prayer for my kids works."*

WE ARE CHANGED THROUGH PRAYER

When we commit to praying for our children, it doesn't just affect them but also goes a long way in affecting us positively too.

> *Prayer changes us. We are transformed in his presence.*
> *We become like who we spend time with.*

We see the early apostles who were illiterates and unlearned men share the gospel with eloquence and boldness because they spent time with God. When we pray we exchange strength with God. We take on His strength for our weakness and we can surpass our expectations as well as those of others. **"Now when** they saw the boldness of Peter and John, and perceived that they were uneducated and untrained men, they marveled. And they realized that they had been with Jesus." Acts 4:13

The essence of God's being begins to overshadow us and we begin to take on His traits and attributes, thus becoming more God-like. We become more sensitive to other people's needs and thus better able to help them. We also become more tolerant and understanding with our kids.

A happy mother shares her testimony of how prayer has been rewarding to her; she says *"Our children believe in God and have confidence in His power to provide, protect, and guide in the right path. We taught them to pray about everything. Even if they needed a pen, it must be given as a prayer request at the family altar or personally prayed about before we buy or give money for purchases"*.

She continues: *"My kids have good insight and revelation of the Word of God. I loved to listen to them share from the Word even while they were quite young and that is one thing I miss so much about them at the daily family altar (now that my nest is empty!). My kids are confident about God's love and present help. I hear them say "Mummy, we love the way you pray for*

*us", "... you prayed mum and it came through"; "...
you are praying and we know these are answers to
your labor in prayers." They know that God hears
mum's prayers because they see the results and see the
peace we enjoy even when we have to wait for a long
time for the things we prayed about. Just a few
examples below. Our firstborn works in a bank and
his section was expected to get in some targeted
amount. He would often call me to help him pray in a
big catch he was after. Our youngest was facing an
examination and she was not confident about her
abilities or preparedness. Right there in the hall
outside this country, before the exams started, she
called for prayers. Our second came out of the doctor's
office during her third trimester for the second baby in
the United States of America (USA) and called me
immediately saying. "Mum begin to pray now....." My
third-born spoke to me before she got married,
"Mummy, I like this guy but I want to be sure if it is
God's will and I want you to pray. You are the only
person I am telling this now." My grandchildren love
me to pray for them. It gives me a lot of joy and hope
that the following generation cannot get lost by God's
grace. Prayer helped my children to be accountable
and to fear God. They were serious with their studies
and have excelled in their chosen careers. They
learned to be honest in financial matters, being
accountable as much as was required of them. They*

are aware that God sees them anywhere, anytime and that has been a huge check that spared me a lot of heartaches. They've learned to pray on their own. That reduced their dependence on me. Building a godly character has been the most rewarding impact. None of my kids struggled with negative peer pressure...none that became very obvious. They were prayerfully taught the Word across many issues of life. Praying for their friends (we encouraged them to have Christian friends)...also has helped them to sustain lasting good relationships. Our parents became family friends with some persons because of praying for children. My children learned to adapt to people of various backgrounds and not to despise people. This had resulted from our family praying for people, relatives, classmates, teachers, friends, neighbors, workers, house-helps, drivers, etc. My mother-in-law once told me that she has never visited a home where the children were as friendly to visitors as my children were. [Both grandmothers knew the Lord and were very prayerful persons, a great heritage we enjoy]. Our home has largely been a peaceful place because my children did not fight, like being physical. Yes, I heard them argue or quarrel sometimes but they did not keep malice (I never noticed any worrisome prolonged malice between my kids or with others in the home). My children are all married now. None of them gave us serious concern over their relationship with the opposite sex before they got married. By God's grace, each one of them is enjoying stable family life. Prayer and the family altar are core values in their homes. Praying is rewarding! So many rewards of prayer captured in this remarkable testimony of a mum and grand-mum. Praise God!

CATALYZE

CHAPTER FOUR

THE PROCESS

Children are a gift from God and they are truly a blessing! **"Behold, children are a heritage from the Lord, The fruit of the womb is a reward."** **Psalm 127:3**

Finding out that we were expecting a child three months after we got married was the best news I had ever heard. I was so excited and expectant. Though as the days progressed, I began to experience the different physical and emotional changes that come with pregnancy and this began to trigger mixed feelings. While the process involved in having a child can be quite challenging, children bring so much joy and happiness that cannot quite be explained. I believe God made it so. Indeed children are gifts, because we welcome their arrival with such joy and excitement that is not quite different from what you experience when you receive a gift from someone who truly loves and cares for you - all you want to do is admire and cherish the gift! After the exhilaration, the reality of caring and raising these little ones dawns on you, which may leave you burdened; however, you should let that burden drive you to pray.

Parenting will be made easier for us when we become more observant of our children in all ramifications and become well informed in the dynamics of their evolvement. This will greatly support and help us aim our prayers more accurately. Most mums take their time to study the maturation process and stages of their unborn child during pregnancy. They learn what to expect at each trimester and how to properly adjust to the changes. This knowledge has helped and supported a lot of mothers like myself to navigate that season of life with little or no difficulties at all. Knowledge releases the grace to work through a process. But unfortunately, most mums do not intentionally continue to study the growth and unfolding of their children from birth through to adulthood. This understanding is also as vital. It consists of discerning and understanding the impact of age progression on the biological, mental, cognitive, emotional, social and spiritual needs of these children. These changes that occur should serve as relevant tools to target your prayers accordingly.

"Like arrows in the hand of a warrior; so are the children of one's youth." Psalm 127:4

Having a basic understanding of these dynamics, will arm you to aim your arrows more accurately. Being privy to some of these information before you ever start having babies or while still having babies gives you an edge to do better. I pray this book will close the knowledge gap for younger people. It will be a delight for me to see that this book helps several other young women in their parenting journey. I know parenting has never been as good as it is now because more young parents have become more intentional about raising their children, but there are still a lot of grounds to cover.

The information shared here in this chapter is not only for the psychologist, child-care practitioners, teachers, school owners but for all mums as well. So while others are experts in their different fields, you and I ought to be experts in our divine assignment as mothers. You may not receive a comprehensive analysis here but a slice will whet your appetite and challenge you to make your own research for more knowledge in these areas.

Different psychology theorists such as Jean Piaget, Lev Vygotsky, Lawrence Kohlberg, and Erik Erikson have defined the stages of growth in childhood and provided ways to understand the development. Recent research has provided significant information regarding the nature of human development. The rendering of these stages differs culturally, sometimes by social institutions, patterns and practices, as well as laws that make up a society. For example, while researchers and professionals usually define the period of early childhood as birth to eight years of age, some western countries such as the United States might consider age five a better endpoint because it corresponds with entry into the cultural practice of formal schooling. In the Nigerian context, early childhood will be from birth to six years of age.

Development is a continuous series of changes that occur in an orderly predictable sequence as a result of advancement and experience. The development of a human being is a continuous process from conception to death. In other words, growth is lifelong. The rhythm of childhood exists within the context of the most universal cycle of all - *birth, youth, maturity, old age, and then death. While the butterfly has the same stages of development as a human, the different stages are easy to tell apart. It looks explicitly distinct at different times in its development. From egg to caterpillar to pupa then butterfly.* These are four stages of development and four different manifestations of the same creature. While human beings reflect the same process too, unlike the butterfly, they do not announce a new stage of development with a new body. It is the same body, but with a slight or drastic increase in size depending on genetic factors. We evolve gradually and the emotional, mental, and psychological changes are inconspicuous as time passes. This physical progression makes it harder for parents to be aware of the changes which their kids are going through.

THE INFANT

The first stage of infancy covers approximately the first two to four weeks of life. It is the shortest developmental period. It is a time for radical adjustment for the newborn. The infant must make four major adjustments to post-natal life which are: temperature changes, sucking and swallowing, breathing, and elimination. At this stage, mums need to uphold their babies in prayer to survive and adjust properly to a world that is different from what they've been accustomed to for nine months. Here mums should emphasize the power of the spoken word. You should start from the first day you learned you were pregnant. God's word spoken from your mouth is a most powerful creative force. The most powerful force at the disposal of the Christian is the power of the spoken word of God.

"Death and life are in the power of the tongue, and those who love it will eat its fruit." Proverbs 18:21

When you learn to take the truths of God's word and speak them out of your mouth, mixing them with the faith in your heart, you unleash the same power that created the whole universe!

"By faith, we understand that the worlds were framed by the word of God, so that the things which are seen were not made of things which are visible." Hebrews 11:3

Creative energy flows freely and change is commanded in those circumstances you speak to. So a pregnant woman should consistently speak words of well-being and victory to herself and to her unborn child. These words are spirits and they have life in them.

"It is the Spirit who gives life; the flesh profits nothing. The words that I speak to you are spirit, and they are life." John 6:63

Remember, your baby is also a spirit, so he or she can hear everything you say and do. During my first pregnancy, any time I was in church and the praise and worship was going on, my daughter would be having her gig in my tummy. Once the drums start rolling, she would start dancing and leaping. I understand clearly when Elizabeth said the child leaped in her. A friend told us the story of a woman who was pregnant in the early 90s and she would consistently speak these words to her unborn baby: "You are bold, beautiful and confident" until the baby turned two years. The result was a little girl who was extremely bold and confident. This baby made an impression because she wasn't strikingly attractive or cute, everyone took note of her not because of her looks, but because of the energy she exuded. She was magnetic. You couldn't help but notice her. We learned later that the mum who was not very good looking must have been dealing with her insecurities and decided her daughter would be different. What this woman did was to impart grace and blessing on her daughter as well as program her for success from birth with the power of the spoken word. Babies can hear us but they can't articulate words. As a mother, you can bless your children with your words. By declaring words over your infant, you are calling the things that be not as though they were.

- ...as it is written, "I have made you a father of many nations" in the presence of Him whom he

believed—God, who gives life to the dead and calls those things which do not exist as though they did. Romans 4;17

BABYHOOD STAGE

As we speak words to our babies, we expect to see what we desire to happen in, for, and through them, we impart blessings on them. I encourage you to speak life, health, strength, soundness of mind, wellness, smartness, wholeness, confidence, adaptability, protection, to your infants. Your infant in a couple of weeks, grows into babyhood and then to early childhood.

CHILDHOOD STAGE

This period in a child's life is characterized by his or her attachment to caregivers to whom the child is dependent. Here the child is learning to take solid foods, learning to walk and talk, learning to control the elimination of body wastes, getting ready to read, learning to distinguish right and wrong, and beginning to develop a conscience. At this stage, your child has begun to develop cognitive abilities, confidence in their body, and is getting conversant with all his or her feelings.

Mums, this stage is crucial and it is the foundation of the formative years of your child. The child's brain is receptive and eager for the stimulation of raw materials where exploration and curiosity to learn occurs naturally. Prayers should be geared toward the proper physical, mental, emotional, social, and spiritual development of the child. Here, your child should be at par with the developmental milestones expected at each age. The child's brain is at a lower vibration of consciousness and the child is said to be at the Theta stage which means active imagination and near hypnosis. This means the child is absorbing everything from his or her environment as his or her reality. Whether we know it or not the child is being programmed by the behavior and responses of the dominant people in their lives at this stage. They just observe and download it into their spirits or subconscious mind. So the question is what are you providing for your child to download? Since the child is at a lower state of consciousness, this is the stage to program the child with truth, virtue, right behavior, powerful words, scriptures, and prayers. The mother spends more time with the child and she is mostly responsible for raising the child at this stage.

You can program your child for kingdom exploits by speaking words that minister grace and life to them, by creating a faith-filled and joy-filled environment for them. ***This is the stage to start praying with them not just praying for them.*** Lay hands on them regularly and declare the word over them; spend worship time with them, read the bible to them, and purchase age-level Bibles and Bible stories for them. Lead them in scripture and affirmative declaration. Take them to church at every church meeting not just on Sundays. Be aware of the child's need at this stage and deal accordingly.

"And these words, which I command thee this day, shall be in thine heart: You shall teach them diligently to your children, and shall talk of them when thou sit in your house, when you walk by the way, when you lie down, and when you rise up. You shall bind them as sign on your hand, and they shall be as frontlets between your eyes. You shall write them on the doorposts of your house, and on your gates." Deuteronomy 6:6-9

Be the first to write on their blank minds and feed them with clear concepts of anything you want them to become. This is the stage of idealizing. Whatever is presented to them as the ideal of life is what they imbibe as the ideal. Here children want to do what mum and dad does.

There was the story of a gangster who had a son whom he loved so much. He would pull out his gun, place it on the table, and go out for all his gangster activities while his son watched with admiration. Meanwhile, he dreamed of a different life for his son. He wanted him to get an education and live a responsible life. One day he asked his son what he would like to be, and the son excitedly told him he wanted to be like his father - a gangster! He expressed his admiration for his dad, as he watched him lead and lord over others. The man was broken and that was the day he changed; he realized his son was being molded by his environment, and that if he did not change, his son would end up just like him – a gangster. You can't be praying your children into rightness, but modelling the wrong things before them. Parenting forces you to step up your game.

THE ADOLESCENT AND THE EARLY TEEN

From late childhood into adolescence and early teens, your child is learning the physical and social skills necessary for building a wholesome attitude towards oneself as a growing organism. Children at this stage learn to get along with age-mates and begin to develop appropriate masculine or feminine social roles associated with their gender. Cognitively, they develop fundamental skills in reading, writing, calculating, concepts necessary for everyday living; they develop a conscience and a sense of morality. Here you begin to teach them to pray for themselves along the lines you have been praying for them before, and you start speaking scriptures into their minds because their will is forming to make choices as their consciousness is being awakened.

Adolescents' desire supervised self-expression. I remember my son would beg us when he was nine years of age to wash the car, polish his father's shoes, and even cook. They can begin to read and explain the scriptures by themselves under supervision. Schedule prayer times for them. The idea here is not to be rigid. We have been more used to the religious practice of morning devotions, but we can have prayer times in the evening as well. While we should work with a schedule, it should remain flexible so that they can enjoy the process. The teenagers gravitate towards achieving new and more mature relations with age-mates of both sexes, understanding a masculine or feminine social role, learning to accept their physical features, and using their body effectively. At this stage too, they learn to accept and achieve socially responsible behavior, as well as emotional independence from parents and other adults. As they exit their teens, they begin to conceive a mind for an economic career, for marriage and for family life. They acquire a set of values and an ethical system as a guide to behavior and they begin to develop their own ideology.

THE LATE TEENS

Mothers should assist teenage children to become responsible and happy adults. What is needed most for teenagers is prophetic interpretation. A mother needs to develop the ability to hear what they are not telling you. Be quick to notice their mood swings and their body language in other to communicate effectively with them. I cannot begin to tell you how many times we have detected something our teenagers were not telling us. You need to engage in spiritual espionage and supervision. You need to be praying for them a lot in the Spirit. At this stage, you need to exercise your faith to believe that they are turning out well, no matter what the physical evidence depicts. Do not allow yourself to get so exasperated or discouraged by what they do that you start destroying what you have been building.

At this stage, they tend to have independent thinking and an experimentation mindset. They may want to blend in with their peers. Do not panic when you see these. Spend your time praying bad friends out of their lives and good friends into their lives. You must use your words to build them up, not to tear them down at this stage. Teach your teenagers to learn to write their own scripture confessions and encourage them to use it often. This practice will help clear the ambiguities that are a common trait at this stage, so they can stay focused. Get them involved in all spiritual activities within the home and in church, and model Christ-likeness to them.

YOUNG ADULTS

Last but not the least is early adulthood, where the children are getting started in an occupation, selecting a mate, learning to live with a marriage partner, starting a family, rearing children, managing a home, taking on civic responsibilities, etc. The interesting thing is that if you have adequately made the spiritual investments of prayer in all forms into your children before this time, they will be living the answers to those prayers at this stage of their lives. The prayer inputs you have made into their lives will define the success of their careers, work, businesses, and choice of a life partner, starting a family, raising their children, and managing their own families as well.

CRACK THE CODE

The link between a mother and a child is profound, and new research suggests a physical connection even deeper than anyone thought before. The profound psychological and physical bonds shared by the mother and her child begin during gestation when the mother is everything for the developing fetus, supplying warmth and sustenance, while her heartbeat provides a soothing constant rhythm.

"Can a woman forget her nursing child, And not have compassion on the son of her womb?" Isaiah 49:15

This scripture stresses the strong and powerful bond a mother shares with her child. It's a code even science is unable to fully crack.

The physical connection between mother and fetus is provided by the placenta - an organ built of cells from both the mother and fetus, which serves as a conduit for the exchange of nutrients, gasses, and wastes. Cells may migrate through the placenta between the mother and the fetus, taking up residence in many organs of the body including the lung, thyroid, muscle, liver, heart, kidney, and skin.

This is insinuating that the cells from the mother integrate into the tissues of the child as a distinct person. This cannot be far from the truth as an unborn child and its mother are connected both physically and emotionally. And if that is so, they are much more connected spiritually! This is because man is a spirit.

"Now may the God of peace himself sanctify you completely; and may your   whole spirit, soul, and body be preserved blameless at the coming of our Lord Jesus Christ." 1 Thessalonians 5:23

The mother's physical state and emotional state can both have an impact on prenatal development. The environment inside the uterus, where the unborn child is developing known as the prenatal environment is linked to the mother's physical, emotional, and spiritual condition. In other words, everything the mother experiences, the baby experiences as well. That's why pregnant women are restricted from certain physical activities that may lead to stress and substances that may cause ill-health. Once the mother is stressed or sick, the baby is stressed or sick too. This connection was created by God Himself to empower the mother's rights and authority over her child. If her physical and emotional condition can adversely affect her baby, then it is much truer that her spiritual temperature and oversight over her child can have a tremendous impact as well.

I have had premonitions on many occasions about my children when they were away from me. Tell me it's the 'mothers' instinct.' Oh yes! There wouldn't be an instinct if the mother is not connected to the child in special ways. Carrying your child for nine months empowers you to build and shape their life. If you can see the power of your unique connection to your child, you will never feel helpless again, but you'll rather use all the powers at your disposal to raise a kingdom giant.

Two main natural factors create this strong bond that is unbreakable and fuels your influence over your child.

1. THE UMBILICAL CORD

When your baby emerges from the womb at birth, he or she is attached to the mother by the umbilical cord. The first thing the doctor or midwife does is severe this cord so that the baby can make it on their own in the world. However, the umbilical cord has significance besides the purely physical. This metaphorical connection to the birth mother will make its influence felt throughout the life of both child and mother. This bond between mother and child is so powerful that no matter how hard outside agents may try to break it, they may even seem to succeed to a certain extent at times, but the connection will stay and re-surface later.

Let's take a brief look at the medical explanation of the purpose of the umbilical cord. The umbilical cord plays a key role in the gestation of the developing fetus. It provides nutrients and oxygenates your baby's blood. It serves as the baby's life-line in the uterus. This, along with the expulsion of the placenta from the womb, reflects the transitory nature of these organs. They both develop to carry out a specific and temporary function. Once fulfilled, these organs are discarded. Given the above-mentioned functions, the umbilical cord is indispensable for embryonic development. Though the physical placenta may be transitory and seems temporary, the spiritual connection remains real and continues to influence the mother to keep her child nourished, fed, and sustained not just physically anymore, but spiritually.

The umbilical cord also physically demonstrates the union between mother and child in its maximum expression. For that reason and many more, mothers are a fundamental pillar in their children's lives. Despite the expulsion and discarding of the placenta with the umbilical cord as the connector, mums need to understand that the invisible connection remains and should be leveraged in prayer. Many mothers report that after childbirth, they knew when their baby was awake even when they were not physically with them. Others know instinctively what the child needs at any given time. Still, others note that their body rhythms seem to naturally adapt to the sleep cycles of their child. That bond does not seem to weaken as children get older. In fact, in many cases, that bond gets stronger. Parents report knowing the instant a child is in trouble or sense that they need to check in on a child who has been quiet for far too long. My friend Rose tells how she knew long before it was uncovered that all was not well with her son in school.

You have most likely heard of the term 'a mother's intuition'. It refers to the fact that mothers seem to sense the moods of their children and can often pick up on minor nuances, such as words not said, to build a clearer picture of what is going on with their children. Since a mother is biologically connected to her child during the pregnancy, it is not a stretch to believe that there were strong energetic connections built between the two as well. While the umbilical cord can be cut, it's more difficult to cut the energetic and spiritual ties that bind them. This then means that the bond between mother and child can be useful while the mother is raising her children, since it helps her to spiritually anticipate their needs and take them to God in prayer. As time passes, the child may begin to notice that he or she can also intuitively sense things about the mother.

2. BREAST FEEDING

"Can a woman forget her suckling child, that she should not have compassion on the son of her womb?" Isaiah 49:15

This scripture makes us understand the strength of connection that develops between a mother and her child at the breast. Here, in as much as God expressed a possibility of a mother forgetting her nursing child, He was emphasizing the strong bond a mother has with a child that could make separation impossible while trying to express man's unreliability in comparison to God's character of dependability.

Breast feeding permanently establishes a connection

between mother and child that both parties can take full advantage of. Growing up, I would hear my mum and other mothers say things like: *"If so-so-and-so person sucked my breast then….!"* What they were trying to express in essence is that they knew they had a powerful influence, to the point of almost hypnosis on their children, because they birthed and breast-fed them. Some of our parents used this power negatively by using it to make unnecessary demands, and when angry, even cursing the child. But we can leverage it and use it positively, because we know better.

Mums, how you think about and speak to your child will make a significant impact on them. Your thoughts as well as your words are creative energy with a powerful force to impact your children for good or for bad. ***Every word you speak to them is a prayer. Every thought toward and about them is a prayer.***

CHAPTER SIX

THE DYNAMICS

"Before I formed you in the womb I knew and approved of you as my chosen instrument; and before you were born I separated and set your apart, consecrating you; and I appointed you as a prophet to the nations." Jeremiah 1:5-6

My friend Rose Ojabo is a middle-aged Christian mum of five children, who shared with me when and how she started to pray for her children. She says: *"I have a system in place for praying for my children which I stumbled into. Before then I was completely clueless about praying intentionally for them. It started when I took in for my first child in 2002. I noticed I was spurting and went to the hospital as a result. After a while the spotting became a heavy flow, there the doctors told me it could lead to a miscarriage if it persisted. It was in that state that I turned to the Lord for intervention. While I was on bed rest, I will lay my hands on my tummy and begin to speak life to her. And the Lord did intervene. After I had her, I was led to pray over her every night. I haven't stopped four other children after".*

Elizabeth Amuta shares her fascinating experience here when she said she started praying for her children before she got married! Hear her: *"I prayed from time to time for the children God would give me. I became pregnant soon after marriage and prayer for the baby on the way and all other kids we would have now became a regular daily item. Every woman who looks forward to motherhood should start praying even before marriage. By praying you are planning well and putting in place your desires (Spirit-led) for your future children".*

The best time to start praying and interceding for your children is when you become aware of the need and importance of it. So if you haven't started already to pray for them, the best time to start would be now! This in essence means that you can start praying for your children long before you even have them.

Iniobong Ebong a mother of four teenagers says: *"I started praying for my children even before I got married. I joined this women's group in my husband's church back then because I use to visit him from Kaduna from time to time. When married women gathered to pray, I would go and join them.*

The pastor's wife used to encourage us singles to join the women pray; she would say, "even if you are not yet married, come and join the women and pray for your children." So this set the tone for me. I valued those prayer times so much that I started praying for my children even before I got married. After marriage, I took in almost immediately. One desire I made known to the Lord after marriage was I wanted a set of twins, and the Lord granted my request. Did you see that? She prayed for a set of twins and God answered. What do you desire? Pray! While pregnant with my babies, I learned to pray for them. I had an encounter with a book called Supernatural Childbirth after I had prolonged labor with my first child. I did not want that to occur again so I dived into the book to build my faith. My mother-in-law was a strong support to me as well".

I remember walking into a bookstore after I had my first baby and coming across the book 'Supernatural Childbirth' as well. Once I scanned through and found it a useful book to build my faith for conception and childbirth, I settled down to read and digest it. It worked for me for my subsequent births so I became a crusader of that book. I have lost count of how many people I gave copies of it to.

Our earlier quoted key text – **Jeremiah 1:5-6** makes

us understand that our children existed in the mind of God long before we ever conceived and birthed them into the earth. A single sister can spend her time interceding for her unborn children long before she meets her husband. By doing this, she leverages the power and efficacy of prayer to shape a future she desires. Those prayers create the right atmosphere into which the children should be born. You will find that the children are practically born into certain graces that begin to play out as they grow. It might just be that they never struggle with what other kids have a hard time with. They will be glaringly different from other children. A great example of such in the Bible was Samuel. Hannah had so religiously and desperately prayed for her child Samuel that he had no option than to turn out the way he did. Remember Samuel grew up in the house of a backslidden priest of God. The two sons of Eli namely Hophni and Phinehas were not the best influence for a young boy growing up, but the prayer price his mum paid year in year out over him even before he was born kept him safe and sound amidst all the temptations to be and to do otherwise. Hannah asked the Lord for Samuel. We can ask the Lord for the kind of children we want long before they are born and even after we give birth to them, we can keep asking God for who they should become. Later on, this was what Hannah had to say:

"For this child I prayed, and the Lord has granted me my petition which I asked of him." 1 Samuel 1:27

Anna, the prophetess, was widowed at her prime and she spent the rest of her life interceding for the birth of the messiah. The prophecy of the messiah had gone out. She could have sat down with folded hands waiting for the manifestation of the messiah as it has been told, but she decided to do something of worth about it and that was to pray. There is a prophecy upon every child we birth whether we know it or not. There is that which has been written concerning them in the Book and we must of necessity ensure that their lives align with what has been written. This can be achieved through prayer.

"Then said I, Lo, I come (in the volume of the book it is written of me,) to do thy will, O God." Hebrews 10:7

Both women, Hannah and Annam did not stop praying for these children until they witnessed the answers to their prayer. Sometimes we start praying and we quit too early, because it seemed we were not seeing the results of our prayers. What if Hannah had quit going to Shiloh that year? The Bible states that she went year in, year out. In other word's she kept praying. You might yet be expecting a child after years of marriage like Hannah and you are contemplating to quit just because your physical eyes haven't seen the child yet; but you might be closer to your miracle than your physical senses can perceive. We need to recognize that even in our spiritual pursuits, the law of compound effect is at work. The Bible states that the testing of our faith works patience. It is through faith and patience that we inherit the promises of God. As we commit to a consistent visit into the spiritual birthing place of prayer daily, our prayers are adding up to create our miracles and results. God will cause us to see the results of our travails and we shall be satisfied in Jesus' Name. Amen! One would imagine how she can make time for prayer in today's busy world. I want to emphasize again that we all are different and are in different circumstances, so you have to find what works for you. It's not a one-size-fits-all situation. I pray while driving, while bathing, cooking and cleaning up. Sometimes when I'm going through my activities for the day and the thought of my children flash through my mind I pick it up from there with a prayer for them.

Rose says consistency has been a huge challenge, however, she has tried to work out a way to meet this obligation of praying for her children. She says: *"I made up my mind to pray over them every day before they went to bed. But there are times I just couldn't because I had a rough day, was angry at them, or completely forgot. There were times I had to travel out of town so the lack of physical contact became a challenge too. So I went back to my heavenly father, who gave them to me, and asked for intervention, and again he did. I studied my days in the week and realized that Thursdays are less busy. So I dedicated Thursday just for them. I wrote their names down in my prayer journal and I'll take each child by name to God. I have seen miracles and deliverances occur by this intentional call to prayer over them. I pray for them daily, I still walk to their rooms to pray over them as I touch them. Since I am not much of a deep sleeper, whenever I wake up at night I quickly do that. But the Thursday prayers have produced the best result so far.*

You are not alone in the struggle to consistently pray, but you can lean on God to grant you wisdom and strength to come up with a unique plan like Rose was able to do. For me I change plans in seasons. I run with what works for me for a season and then I create a new plan to adapt to a new season. There was a season I prayed one day in the week for all of them, another season I prayed for each child on a particular day of the week.

Elizabeth Amuta says: *"I am open to prayer anytime, anywhere, praying with my understanding and in tongues. Though my times of devotion in the morning and evening would usually include all or some of my children, I could find myself praying anytime. Good communication with them has also helped my ability to be definite in my prayers for them. The help of the Holy Spirit has been an amazing experience because I enjoy a lot of peace after interceding in tongues. Awesome!* Rose found a schedule and routine that works perfectly for her, while Elizabeth says she is open to prayer anytime as the Spirit leads.

So I would advise, that you go with what works for you but make sure you are praying. What matters is consistency. You can pick a day in a week for each child, or you can pick a day in a week to fast and pray for all your kids. But don't bite more than you can chew. Start simple first. It could even be 15 minutes of consistent prayer time weekly. If you attempt something big from the onset and you are unable to follow through, it will be demotivating. So what we want to do is get on a routine we can keep. There is power in consistently praying for your children. Sometimes it may seem that our prayers are not receiving answers, but we need to understand what God promises us when we pray. Don't give up on them. Just as you constantly love and would care for them, allow consistency to characterize your prayers for them.

With the guide I have provided in the later pages of this book you can pray regularly for your children. There were times I was tempted to give up praying for my kids because it didn't seem my prayers were working. Their challenging traits seemed to get worse, they would get me upset, and I would get wary of calling upon God. But I knew better, so at such times, I had to keep on. As believers, not doubters, mums we have a basic call to pray without ceasing. **"Pray without ceasing." 1 Thessalonians 5:17**

"Ask and it will be given to you, seek and you will find, knock and it will be opened to you. For everyone who ask receives, and he who seeks finds, and he who knocks it will be opened." Matthew 7:7 -8

We are guaranteed answers to our prayers when we make our requests. If you do not receive answers, it's not God's problem; you either did not ask or you asked amiss. **"You do not have because you do not ask. You ask and do not receive because you ask amiss." James 4:2b-3**

Knowing that God answers our prayer should encourage us not to relent in going into the secret place with confidence to talk to God about our children. He doesn't just promise to answer us but He promises to hear us when we pray in line with His will. God's word is His will and His will is His word. So we need to tailor our prayers according to His word.

"Now this is the confidence that we have in him, that if we ask anything according to his will, he hears us. And if we know that he hears us, whatever we ask we know that we have the petitions that we have asked of him."
John 5:14-15

Praying with what God has said in the Bible about your children will guarantee answers. This is why I have provided some resources such as scriptures, confessions and affirmations we can use in praying for our children in Chapter 8 of this book.

CHAPTER SEVEN

THE CONSEQUENCES

Prayerlessness is a sin. While some people can admit that their prayer life is weak and ineffective, it is important to know we sin when we do not pray at all. It is pure unbelief and an affront on God not to pray. It is your pride saying, "I can do it all by myself, so please God, get out!"

Moreover, as for me, God forbid that I should sin against the Lord in ceasing to pray for you: but I will teach you the good and the right way: 1 Sam 12:23

"But he who doubts is condemned if he eats, because he does not eat from faith: for whatsoever is not from faith is sin." Romans 14:23

"But without faith it is impossible to please him: for he who comes to God must believe that he is, and that he is a rewarder of those who

diligently seek him." Hebrews 11:6

It is a sin not to pray, because of all that prayer can accomplish. By not praying we dam and hinder the channels through which mighty blessings could and should be flowing to us. When we do not pray for our children, we do not only deprive them but also ourselves, the family, and the society of the blessing of whole and sound citizens. We rob God's kingdom of grounded and established saints who will carry on the baton of light into a dark world.

Some possible consequences of not paying the prayer price are:

UNFULFILLED DESTINIES

"For I know the thoughts that I think toward you, says the Lord, thoughts of peace and not of evil. To give you a future and a hope. Then you will call upon me and go and pray to me, and I will listen to you." Jeremiah 29:11

God has a blueprint for everyone born into this earth to actualize. But we can't possibly fulfill destiny without hitches because of the presence of Satan, the opposer. We will find it difficult to overcome these hitches if we do not pray. Even with prayer we still encounter obstacles.

After God had revealed His plans for Israel through Jeremiah, the next thing He would say is, **"...then you will call upon me and pray and I will listen."** God expects mothers to war 'a good warfare' with the prophecies he has given concerning their children. God has a plan for our children. In fact, he has a purpose for their individual lives. But His intentions are not going to happen automatically. You should be willing to pay a prayer price for your children's destiny to be fulfilled according to God's plan. If you fail to pay the price of travailing for your children, chances are that they may rarely actualize the fullness of glory that God designed for them.

In this dispensation of man, evil grows on its own, but good has to be cultivated.

This means you are responsible for your results. You have to become intentional through prayer, if you don't want your kids to fail. If you fail to pray for your children, your children could fail in life. Through prayer, Jabez was able to change the trajectory of his life and his destiny. He name meant 'born in sorrow,' so I guess negative occurrences were trailing his life. One day he decided to cry out unto God for a change, and his life was transformed.

In the Book of Acts Chapter 12, we see James the

Apostle held up in prison, and eventually, he was beheaded. Peter was arrested as well but later released supernaturally by the help of God. What Peter had that James didn't have were people who prayed for him. If you don't give yourself to praying for your children, their destinies could be cut short like James' when the 'Herods' of life attack them. The scriptures say, "While men slept, the enemy came to sow tares..."

Eve did not excel in this assignment at all. The proof is that the first sibling rivalry occurred in her home which resulted in Cain killing Abel because of jealousy and envy. Abel's life was cut short because a mother failed to pray, and Cain became a murderer who was ostracized from his home.

We see another person in scripture, who didn't fulfill destiny because perhaps his mother didn't see a need to pray his destiny through. Samson's father was a man named Manoah who hailed from Torah of the tribe of the Dan. His mother's name was not mentioned but we are told she was barren and had no children until the Angel of the Lord appeared to her and told her she was going to become pregnant and bear a son. Her encounter was very spectacular and prophecies concerning her son were quite detailed.

"She may not eat anything that comes from the

vine, nor may she let drink wine or similar drink, nor eat any thing unclean: all that I commanded her let her observe." Judges 13: 14

Samson's destiny was to deliver the Israelites from the hands of the Philistines. While Samson's mother kept all the rules when she was pregnant for Samson, and even after he was born till he became older. It seems that at a point she lost touch with praying for her son. Instead of her losing control over her son at a point when he no longer heeded their counsel, she could have interceded for his restoration. We see Samson being manipulated by his wife to reveal the meaning of his riddle, and also by Delilah to reveal the secret of his power which was a sacrilege. His mother's prayers could have helped him in his moments of weakness. Our prayers can go beyond our feet and words to effect the changes we desire in our children, to stop Satan from interrupting God's will for their lives.

SATANIC VICTORIES

The main assignment of the devil is to steal, to kill, and to destroy! **"The thief does not come, except to steal, and to kill, and to destroy:..."John 10:10a**

When Jesus was about to be born, Satan was bent on

stopping his entrance into this world by entering into Herod who then gave a command to kill every child that was less than two years old. If he had succeeded to kill Jesus, Satan would have taken the victory. The victory does not belong to the devil, but to the Lord. But if we fail to pray for our children and the devil messes up their lives, Satan will take the victory.

A good example is this wealthy and generous woman who provided a resting place for Elisha every time he came to their town. God had used the grace upon His servant to give her a miracle child. On this particular day, the boy was with his father and he was struck by sickness, he began to yell his head out, and the father, instead of praying for his son, asked that the boy be taken to the mother. Perhaps he was so sure that the mother was going to exercise her faith and authority in God; rather she did nothing until the boy died. **"And the child grew. Now it happened one day he went out to his father, to the reapers. He said to his father, "My head, My head!" So he said to a servant, carry him to his mother. When he had taken him and brought him to his mother, he sat on her knees till noon, and then died."2 Kings 4:18-20**

Here we see a mother who was clueless and careless. She could have prayed for her son and he would not have died. She could have reached out to other mothers like her, or her man of God when she realized the situation was getting out of hand; but to do nothing, to not fight is to relinquish power and victory to the enemy. When we fail to pray Satan seems stronger and he gains the victory. Can you imagine that she was consistently praying for this boy? Satan would possibly have tried but God would have averted the affliction. The enemy will come to destroy our seed, but are we going to give him a chance? While we have Pastors we can call upon in times of distress as she did later, know that as a believer and child of God you have direct access to God as well as the right to ward off the schemes of Satan against your seed.

We don't have to wait for emergencies where we begin to run around for help. It is the great man of God, John Wesley who said that God will do nothing upon the earth except men pray. If our children encounter academic difficulties or they are faced with health challenges or their marriages are troubled or they have a hard time getting a Job, Satan will be happy. It is our duty to refuse to let him have that victory.

MEDIOCRITY

Failing to pray for our kids will make them end up being average kids. Samuel became an excellent prophet because his mother prayed. Our kids will perform below average, if we do not labor in prayer for them. It is obvious to the people who had prayerful mothers, how good their lives eventually turned out. I heard the story of an internationally well-known preacher who is doing very well in ministry. His ministry spans the globe with signs and wonders following. When asked the secret, he said a key reason was the prayers of his mum; his mum had zealously and consistently prayed for him, even before he knew the Lord.

HEARTACHE

If our kids don't turn up well, it will break our hearts. We might think they are small now, and that we have all the time to postpone praying for them until later. But their pains and sufferings usually become our heartaches. Imagine that your child fails in school, graduates from school but never gets a job, is past the age of marriage but still unmarried, is suffering from an addiction, or is married but finding no fruit of the womb. Imagine your child being trapped in situations that make them backslide from the faith, and you hear that they are no longer serving God. All these heartaches can be avoided through prayers.

When Rebekah decided to scheme for Jacob to receive the birthright rather than pray, she initiated a series of heartaches for her and her entire family. Jacob was compulsorily exiled for fear of his brother's wrath. Rebekah would lose her son to unnecessary hard work and labor because she was unwilling to war "a good" warfare with the prophecies about her children. Once Jacob was taught to lie and cheat by his mother, he continued to lie and cheat his way through everything until he encountered God and God changed him. We are not aware of a mother in the life of Hophni and Phinehas. I believe that if a mother's nurture, discipline, and prayers were present in their lives they would have turned up better. They were practically a disgrace and embarrassment to their immediate family and the entire community. They were manipulators, oppressors, fornicators, dishonest, and they practically desecrated the temple of God. You can see how they ended.

RAISING PRAYING KIDS THROUGH A PRAYER ALTAR AND PRAYER LIFE

While it is fantastic and beneficial to pray for our children, the balance will be that as they grow older, you begin to pray with them by raising a prayer altar in the home where the family gathers to pray. By doing this we teach them how to pray. We speak loudly to them that the invitation to come to God's presence is open and that we are entirely dependent on God for everything.

My son had a doctor's appointment one morning. This particular clinic is usually crowded with patients on the days when the clinic opens. So we had to be up early, and at 6:30 am we were on our way. To get ready and be on our way that early meant we were up at 5 am. Truth is that we could not be part of the family prayer time. But realizing that our trip was going to be up to a 45 minutes' drive I asked that we use the time to pray together. And oh it was a refreshing time, though a few times my son would doze off and I would have to tap him.

The more we pray together with them, the more they learn the art of prayer. Learning is effective when the learner is involved. Tell me and I forget, teach me and I may remember, involve me and I learn. Prayer is the most important communication we can have. It is communion with God and cannot be compared to any conversation with friends, associates or family. Prayer goes beyond asking but extends to fellowship with our creator God. Praying is the best spiritual habit we can teach our kids. ***If they can learn to***

pray, you can go to sleep. Because we can be busy, we should always create a schedule that works for us. There isn't anywhere in scriptures where a particular place is taught to be mandatory for prayer. We know that oftentimes when Jesus prayed he went to a solitary place. Also, there is no posture that the Bible insists we must take to pray. While kneeling and bowing is the posture associated with prayer and worship we are not restricted to them. In today's fast, busy and mobile world, if every time you pray you have to kneel, then you will not be able to pray most times. ***The more we spend time praying together with our children, the better they get at praying and the more they enjoy praying.***

- Pray with them on the move. When driving them to or back from school. Utilize driving time and catch a few minutes of prayer.
- Make prayer time fun. Don't make it burdensome. My husband tells the story of how he hated devotion time because he was woken up as early as 5 am. This interrupted his sleep. While prayer may not be convenient we need to understand that a child's brain requires the right conditioning.
- Direct every request they make or family need to a prayer point. Don't make them think you are the superman that makes all things happen, but that God is really the super fixer and the super

provider. By always saying let's pray about it, or let's ask God about it, we create that impression.

- Share testimonies of answered prayers with them. Sharing testimonies will boost and build their faith in God's willingness to hear them and His ability to respond to them. Wow! What a legacy to raise children who love to pray and have developed a habit of praying.

May God help us to raise praying kids!

CHAPTER EIGHT

PRAYER RESOURCES

To effectively pray, you need the right tools. The word of God should be the basis for our prayers. Our prayers are guaranteed to arrive at heaven's gates and be given express attention if we pray according to the will of God. God's word is His will. All you need to do is to find out the promises of God in the scriptures for your children and then, turn them into declarations, prayers of faith and supplication. When we do this, we show that we are in agreement and in partnership with God.

"Now this is the confidence that we have in him, that, if, we ask anything according to his will he hears us; and if we know He hears us, whatever we ask, we know that we have the petitions that we have asked of him."1 John 5:14-15

Something else you need to understand is that many unanswered prayers are a result of not praying in alignment with God's will or praying the wrong types of prayer. There are different kinds of prayers in the word of God, and in each situation, you have to deploy the kind of prayer that fits the need. When it comes to praying for your children, you are meant to invoke your covenant with God for them, which is called the prayer of supplication. Paul spoke about this kind of prayer in his epistles to the Ephesians and Colossians.

"Praying always with all prayer and supplication in the Spirit, being watchful to this end with all perseverance and supplication for all the saints." Ephesians 6:18

"Epaphras, who is one of you, a bond servant of Christ, greets you, always laboring fervently for you in prayers, that you may stand perfect and complete in all the will of God."Colossians 4:12

For instance, you do not begin to intercede for your child's healing or health. Intercessory prayer is when you are praying for someone who has no covenant with God, but supplication is when you plead your covenant for your children. In supplication prayer, you pray the same covenant scriptures over and over again until you see them stand perfect and complete in all the will of God. Hallelujah! I have provided a scripture-based Prayer Guide to assist you in your prayer time and in praying right. It captures scriptures addressing most areas of your child's life. I have included faith confessions and affirmations.

RESOURCE BANK:

1. HEALTH AND HEALING

Father, I commit my children's health to You. I pray that as my children will grow in wisdom to adore and serve You with their undivided attention, that they will enjoy your promises of health in their bodies and strength in their bones. I declare by faith in the written word of God that my children serve you, so every food they eat is blessed and it nourishes their bodies. They shall not be inflicted or afflicted by any of the diseases of this world. My children shall not be weak, frail, or ailing from sickness. They continually enjoy health in their bodies as their souls prosper.

I declare that my child's body is now the sacred Temple of the Holy Spirit who lives in me and in them. They no longer belong to themselves for they have been bought at the price of Jesus' shed blood. I decree that their bodies are God's vehicle here on earth, meant to glorify God and to accomplish His purposes here on earth. Sickness does not glorify, so it will not habitat, live, or reside in any of their bodies in Jesus name.

I declare my child's body is healed from inside out, from every disease. I stand on the finished works of Christ sacrifice and I declare that he took every sickness (mention it) trying to afflict my child's body and he bore their disease on the cross. It greatly delights me, that Jesus was stricken, smitten and afflicted by God for our sake, he was wounded for our transgression and bruised for our guilt and iniquities, the chastisement meant to bring me and my child peace and wellbeing was laid upon him, and with the stripes that wounded him, and my child is healed and made whole! I take his/her healing in Jesus' name! He/she (Child's name) is made whole in Jesus' name! My child rises from this sickbed in Jesus' name!

I rebuke all kinds of fever, sore throat, all manner of infections, Flu, colds, cough, sickle cell anemia, jaundice, sight and hearing impairment, chicken-pox, measles, mumps, rickets, mental disorders, physical disability, learning disabilities, kidney, lungs and heart issues in the name of Jesus! I refuse them on my child! I resist sickness and disease and command it to leave my child's body. I pray Lord as my family dwell in your secret place and abide under your shadow, that we will find a refuge and a fortress in you. As we put our trust in you, I ask that you will deliver us from the snare of the fowler and any outbreak of deadly diseases. I declare that it shall not come near us in Jesus' name.

Scripture references: Proverbs 3:7-8, Exodus 23:25, Psalm 105:37, 3 John 1: 2, I Corinthians 6:19-20, Exodus 15:26, Deuteronomy 7:14-15, Psalms 103:3, Matt 8:17, Isaiah 53:4-5

2. FOR PREGNANT MUMS

With hands placed on your tummy declare: Lord, you are forming my baby in my womb and have covered him or her with your hands. My baby abides under the watchful eyes of the heavenly father. I plead the blood of Jesus over my unborn baby. I stand on the word of God to obtain the promises for my baby. My baby is shielded from all the disease, malformation, deformation, or any disorder streaming from my biological bloodline. His or her growth and development are unhindered. I declare my baby is whole and healthy, there is nothing missing or broken in his/her body. He/She is perfectly formed physically, mentally, emotionally, physiologically.

I love and serve the Lord, therefore every food and drink I eat during this pregnancy is blessed! It nourishes and flourishes me and my baby. I come against any and every health risk associated with this pregnancy. I shall not lose my baby through miscarriage or any means before he/she is full term. I declare that my womb and cervix are strong and healthy to accommodate my baby till full term. My amniotic fluid is the perfect amount to sustain my baby. My blood pressure stays within the perfect limit during and even after this pregnancy, I resist gestational diabetes, infections, pre-eclampsia, pre-term labour, stillbirth, and any other complications. I decree that they shall not be associated with me in the name of Jesus! It is when the fullness of time comes that I shall bring forth; like the Hebrew woman that I am, I will deliver my baby smoothly and swiftly without sorrow and complications in the name of Jesus!

FOR THE FRUIT OF THE WOMB

Fruitfulness is a fundamental human right established in Genesis 1:26-28.This simply means God has empowered and equipped every human to be fruitful and to reproduce. Taking it one step further, God has enacted a covenant of fruitfulness with those who fear Him and who chose to serve him. The Patriarchs like Abraham, Isaac and Jacob had a record of all kinds of fruitfulness including the fruit of the womb even when it seemed there natural hindrances to conception. Every woman who experienced a delay in childbirth in the bible eventually had a baby or more except Micah who despised God. Ultimately, delays and disruptions happen for us not to us , and in the end God is glorified. With these words of exhortation, I encourage you to war a good warfare with the promises provided in scriptures about fruitfulness. Here are a few you can begin with.

- **Leviticus 26:9:**For I will look on you favorably and make you fruitful , multiply you , and confirm my covenant with you.
- **Psalm 127:3-5:** Behold, children are an heritage from the Lord; The fruit of the womb is a reward. Like arrows in the hand of a warrior, so are the children of one's youth. Happy is the man who has his quiver full of them: They shall not be ashamed, but shall speak with their enemies in the gate.
- **Psalm 128:3:** Your wife shall be like a fruitful vine in the very heart of your house, Your children like olive plants all round about your table.
- **Genesis 17:20:** And as for Ishmael, I have heard you: Behold, I have blessed him and will make him fruitful, and will multiply him exceedingly: He shall beget twelve princes and I will make him a great nation. If God will bless Ishmael, he would much more bless Isaac of which you and I belong.
- **Gen 1: 12:** And the earth brought forth grass, the herb that yields seed, according to its kind, and the tree that yields fruit, whose seed is in itself

according to its kind.

- **Gen 1: 28:** Then God blessed them and God said to them 'Be fruitful and multiply: fill the earth and subdue it.
- **Gen 35:11:** "I am God Almighty, Be fruitful and multiply; a nation and a company of nations shall proceed from you couple and Kings shall come from your body.
- **Psalm 113:9:** You grant the barren woman a home, like a joyful mother of children.
- **Isaiah 29:17:** Is it not yet a very little while, till Lebanon shall be turned into a fruitful field, and the fruitful field shall be esteemed as a forest.
- **Genesis 26:22:** ..So he called its name Rehoboth, because he said, "For now the Lord has made room for us, and we shall be fruitful in the Land.
- **Luke 1:37:** For with God nothing will be impossible.
- **1 Samuel 1;21-22:** And Elkanah knew Hannah his wife, and the Lord remembered her. So it came to pass in the process of time that Hannah conceived and bore a son and called his name Samuel, saying "Because I have asked for him from the Lord."

LET US PRAY

I believe God has given me an enormous ability to reproduce and bring forth after my kind.I decree that my reproductive system comes alive now. For my God quickens the dead and calls the things that be not as though they were, so in the same vain I express my creative ability to say, "I am fruitful." I speak life to my uterus, my ovaries and my fallopian tubes. They are revived and restored to function effectively and efficiently. That same Spirit who raised Jesus from the dead quickens my reproductive organs and my system, and that of my husband to work and produce life. Every defect be miraculously healed and restored by the power of God in Jesus name.

Lord I ask that you would graciously give me children, because you are the giver of children. Rejoice over me to do me good and to multiply me. Father make room for me this year. Let this year be my Rehoboth year. For with you nothing shall be impossible. Like Hannah, Sarah , Rachel and Elizabeth, remember me, grant to me the child and children I have asked for. Send help from your sanctuary, and grant me the needed support. Give me the desires of my heart (mention your specific desire). Make me a mother who is like a vine planted by the waters, one who is fruitful and full of branches by reason of your mercy and grace. I exercise my authority in Christ and come against bareness, miscarriages, infant mortality, still births, demonic manipulations, medical complications, low sperm count etc. Father give me peace that transcends my present situation, fill me with joy unspeakable and full of Glory, and strengthen me in faith like Abraham to keep giving you glory, being fully persuaded that what you have promised you are able to perform. Lord help me to rest in your promises like Sarah. I pray to be courageous and not discouraged, to be joyful in hope, patient in affliction and faithful in prayer in Jesus Name.

3. SALVATION AND RIGHTEOUSNESS

I declare that all my children (call their names) shall be Disciples of Christ. They are taught, indoctrinated, discipled, trained, and drilled by the Lord Himself. They are willingly obedient, yielding, and submissive to His will, and great is their peace and undisturbed composure.

My children are established, grounded, deep-rooted, vested, and entrenched in righteousness. They conform to God's will and order. By my prayers, I birth their consecration, anointing, zeal, baptisms, ordination travailing in the Spirit until Christ is formed in them. My children hunger and thirst after righteousness and they shall always be filled. They earnestly desire pure spiritual milk and continue to be nurtured and fed by it. My children grow in the things of God. They walk in truth.

I declare my covenant with God over my children, (call them by name). They shall all be partakers of the Spirit of God upon me and their dad. I declare by covenant, that God's word in our mouth shall not depart from their mouth or that of their children in the name of Jesus. Lord, I pray that you will put your law within them and on their hearts as they grow up. Father, I pray that my children will be saved when they are old enough to make a conscious decision by themselves. I declare that they belong to Christ. I banish ungodliness from the generation you have begun to perpetuate through me. I declare that I and my household are believers in the Lord Jesus Christ.

Father, I know that salvation is not by might or power; I can't force them to serve you neither can they save themselves, so I ask that you will save them by your right arm and the light of your countenance, because of your mercy and favor. Deal with them not according to their shortcoming or sins but have mercy on them. Father cause them to understand the salvation that comes by faith through grace, that which is not dependent on their works but that is a gift from God through Christ.

I pray for their souls, that the light of the gospel will shine through and bring them to genuine repentance from sin. Let your Spirit hover over them when they listen to their Sunday school teachers or when they open up your Word by themselves to read day by day. Let your light shine upon their hearts and in our home. May it penetrate the dark corners and expose what is hidden. Remove every blind spot that will try to hinder their salvation. Bring order to every disordered aspect of their life. Fill up the empty places of their lives with your beauty and life. Lord, shape their life into something beautiful for your glory. Elucidate their eyes to see you and fill their life with your good gifts.

O Lord, give my children the faith to depend on your promises and to lay hold of them. I ask that their faith be counted for righteousness just like Abraham's was. Father help me not to be a stumbling block to my children's salvation and dedication to the Lord. I shall not entice them or hinder them in right conduct or thought in the name of Jesus. Help me to bring them to Jesus in every way.

Scripture reference: Isaiah 54:13-14, 59:21, Psalm 44:3, Acts 16:31-33, Galatians 4:19, I Peter 2:2-3, 3 John1:4, Jeremiah 3:15, Matt 18:2-6, Mark 10:13

4. PRAYER FOR SPIRITUAL GROWTH

Father Lord, I pray and ask for my children (mention names) that you will keep every promise you've made to me about them. Since your love is constant and endless, I ask you Lord, to finish every good thing that you've begun in them. May they stay pure by living in your word and walking in its truth. I pray for them to grow up to be strong, sturdy men and graceful, beautiful daughters royally fashioned as for a palace. May they burn with love and be addicted to Jesus more than drugs, premarital sex, wrong friends, movies, social media, pornography, and material things. Cause them to grow to understand that they have been bought with a price. I declare that they run from all ambitions and lusts of youth and chase after all that is pure. I decree that they are obsessed with what builds up their faith and deepens their love, and holiness has become their pursuit. I declare that my children are consistently living their lives in the way of truth.

I pray for my children to desire the sincere milk of the word of God, that they may grow thereby and soon mature to understand the revelation of righteousness, that their spiritual senses will begin to perceive heavenly matters and grow by experience to understand what is truly excellent and what is evil and harmful.

I declare that like Samuel, my children grow in stature and favor with God and men. I pray that they grow daily in the grace and knowledge of our Lord and Savior Jesus Christ. May they be planted, rooted, and established in the faith; may they grow to bear fruits of service to God and become soul-winners in the kingdom.

I pray that my children's hearts will be receptive to God's word. I declare that their hearts are good ground which keeps the word and bears fruit with patience. I pray for my child/children as they grow to love and serve you, may they not be distracted by the cares of this world or the deceitfulness of riches, or the pleasures of this life disabling them from being fruitful in Jesus name.

I declare that they have spiritual pastors and teachers after your own heart that will feed them with true and accurate knowledge and who will teach them in all understanding and judgment.

I pray for my children, that they may be filled with the full knowledge of your will in all spiritual insight into your ways and purposes. Cause them to be able to understand and discern spiritual things. I pray that Christ be found, formed, and fashioned in them in Jesus' name.

Scripture Reference: Psalms 119:9,138:8, 144:12, John 21:15, 2Timothy 2:22, 3 John 1:4, Heb. 5:12, I Peter 2:2, 1 Samuel 2:26, 2 Peter 3:18, Jeremiah 12:2, Luke 8:14-15, Colossians 1:9-10, 2:6-7, Psalm 92:12-14

5. GUIDANCE AND PROTECTION

Lord, give my children eyes to see the hidden dangers in what may look good on the surface as my children move out of our home and into the world. By your mercy drag them to safety from danger. I pray that your mercy overflow to overcome their compromises and to outweigh the negative influences of their surroundings.

Father God, order their steps into opportunities. Be their shepherd so that they will never want, make them lie down in green pastures. Guide them to flourish and to excel in all their undertakings. Give them acumen and perception beyond their years, to wisely figure out and appraise opportunities that are presented to them.

O Lord I pray that you will keep me and my household by your power; hide me and mine in the hollow of your hands. Father, you are the defender of the poor and the fatherless, arise and defend my children from oppressors and their oppression.

O Lord preserve their ways and keep them from the evil path, as they access your sound wisdom, Help them walk in knowledge and integrity. I declare that you give your angels charge over my children to keep them in your hands, bear them up lest at any time they dash their foot against a stone. Lord as my children fear you and put their trust under your wings, may you be their strong confidence and refuge.

I declare by faith that my family dwells in the shelter of the Most High, and we abide under the shadow of the Almighty! So I say concerning my family that the Lord is our refuge and our fortress, our God, and in him we trust. I pray that you will deliver my children from the hidden traps of Satan, and the deadly pestilence. Cover them with your pinions, and let them find refuge under your wings. Let your faithfulness be their shield and buckler.

They shall not fear the terror of the night nor the arrow that flies by day, nor the pestilence that stalks in darkness, nor the destruction that wasted at noonday. A thousand may fall at their side, ten thousand at their right hand, but it will not come near them. They will only look with their eyes and see the recompense and reward of the wicked, because I have made the Lord my dwelling place—the Most

High, who is my refuge—no evil shall be allowed to befall my children, no plague shall come near their tent. For you oh Lord has commanded your angels concerning them, to guard them in all their ways.

In the hands of angels my children are carried, they shall not strike their foot against a stone. They will tread on the lion and the adder, the young lion and the serpent they will trample underfoot. "Because they hold fast to you in love, you will deliver them always and you will protect them, because they know your name. Whenever they call upon you, you will answer them; you will be with them in trouble and you will always rescue them. Lord satisfy them with long life and show them your salvation in Jesus name."

Scripture Reference: 1 Peter 1:5, Hebrews 11:23, Psalm 82:3, Luke 4:10-11, Psalm 36:7, Proverbs 14:26, Psalm 91:1-11, Psalm 23.

6. CHARACTER DEVELOPMENT

Father, I thank you because through your love you have chosen my children and have given them a new kind of life. I pray for my children that they will reciprocate the deep love and concern you have for them, by being tenderhearted, showing mercy and kindness to others. As siblings may they love each other, be gentle and ready to forgive; never holding grudges against each other. May they always remember, that you forgave them, and so extend that forgiveness to others. May they embrace your love to guide their lives and may they stay together in perfect harmony. O Lord, I pray that my children grow to be Christ-like and that they increase in understanding of your desire for them to help others with the gifts, talents, and abilities you have blessed them with.

I declare that my children will not be destabilized by problems and trials, but that they will rather be empowered, knowing that the challenges help us learn to be patient. Cause them to grow in the strength of character, as they learn to trust you more each time until finally their hope and faith become strong and steady. Help them to be able to hold their heads high no matter what happens, and to know that all is well because they know how dearly you love them. I pray that in trying times they may feel your warm love everywhere within them, because you have given them the Holy Spirit to fill their hearts with your love.

I pray that they will not get tired and discouraged, nor give up on doing what is right; and may they reap a harvest of blessings for the good seeds they sow.

Oh Lord, I ask that my children will submit to the control of the Holy Spirit, so that he will produce the fruits of love, joy, peace, patience, kindness, goodness, faithfulness, gentleness, and self-control in them. May they be willing and learn to relinquish their natural desires where necessary, to pick up their cross and follow the leading of the Holy Spirit, not necessarily looking for popularity and honors which leads to jealousy and hard feelings, but seeking to honor Christ in all they do.

I pray that my child will grow to become patient and godly, gladly letting you have your way. I pray for them that they will remember to fix their thoughts on what is true, good, and right. May their focus stay on things that are pure and lovely, and may they be willing and able to dwell on the fine, good things in others.

Father God, cause my children to learn how to be abased and how to abound, to know how to get along happily whether they have much or little, to live on almost nothing or with everything fully supplied without losing their focus. I pray that they will learn and understand the secret of contentment in every situation.

I pray for them today, asking you to cleanse their

hearts from evil thoughts, and that you fill them with thoughts of the beauty of Christ. Help them to see the ways they have broken your commands, and lead them into repentance. Rid them of deceit, envy, and greed, make them men and women of integrity. Transform any lustful desires into eagerness for your transforming work. Humble them in whatever way you have to. Transform their foolishness into the wisdom that comes from being joined to Christ. **Scripture Reference: Romans 13:14, Colossians 3:12-14,Romans 8:29, Ephesians 2:10, Romans 5:3-5, Galatians 6:7-8, Philippians 4:8, Galatians 5:22, Romans 7:1-25, 2 Peter 16-12**

7. FRIENDSHIP AND PEER INFLUENCE

I declare and I decree that my children shall not walk with fools. They shall only keep company with the wise. I begin to decide their association in the spirit now. I separate them from fools and from folly, from minds that plan iniquity; from wrong, manipulative and negative peer influences and pressures; from people with profane ungodliness and those who speak error concerning the Lord in Jesus name.

I pray for my children not to be connected to an unfaithful person who disguises themself as a friend, or an angry and furious man. I pray that their feet be kept far from any association that will influence and lure them to do evil, and may they never consent to misleading peer pressures in Jesus name.

I pray that the Lord protect them from the path of the wicked, that they may not walk in their ways. I pray that my children would choose their friends carefully. Order the steps of good and godly people into their lives, those who will become huge blessings to them.

I declare that my children shall attract and keep company with friends who love them, sharpens them, stand by them through thick and thin, those who build them up and who celebrate them.

I disconnect them from sexually immoral people, idolaters, covetous people, drunkards, smokers, drug addicts, and extortionist. I pray that they will have a discerning spirit to separate good friends from fake and bad ones.

I declare and pray that my children will hold a higher standard than the world around them. They shall be approved as excellent, pure, and blameless in character and conduct. I declare and pray, my children develop in character so they will excel in Godly value.

Scripture Reference: James 4:4, Proverbs 22:24, Job 34:8, 1Cor 5:11, Proverbs 13:20, 1:10,

4:14-15, Psalm 1:1-2, 1 Cor. 15:33, Romans 12:2, Proverbs 12:26, 27:17, 17:17, 11:14, Isaiah 32:6, 2 Cor. 8:7-8

8. PRAYER FOR SOUNDNESS OF MIND

I declare that God has not given my children the spirit of cringing fear, timidity, or cowardice but that He has given them a spirit of power, of love, and of a calm, well-balanced mind, and of discipline and self-control. They are as bold as a lion. They are confident in God's ability manifesting through them. They possess a sound, coherent, well-grounded mind that thrives emotionally, socially, and mentally. They are free from any personality or mental disorders in the name of Jesus! I declare that my children focus and meditate on things that are true, noble, just, pure and lovely; things of good report and virtues things. I pray that as they interact with scriptures, their minds are renewed and that they are able to prove for themselves what is good, acceptable and the perfect will of God. I declare that they have the mind of Christ. We declare that they are free from anxiety, depression, conduct disorder, attention deficit, hyperactivity disorder, obsessive compulsive disorder, Phobias, insomnia, personality disorders, suicidal thoughts in Jesus name.

I pray that they will continue to experience God's

peace, which is far more wonderful than the human mind can understand. May this peace keep their thoughts and their hearts quiet and at rest as they trust in Christ Jesus.

I pray that my children will grow in the mindset and motivation of Christ. Lord, supernaturally unlock my children's understanding to receive revelation and insights of the scriptures, life lessons, and relationship dynamics in Jesus name.
Scripture Reference: Philippians 4:13, 4:6-8, 2 Tim 1:7, Romans 12:2, I Corinthians 2:16, Ephesians 4:23, Philippians 2:5, 4:7, Luke 24:45

9. PRAYER FOR DESTINY CLARITY AND FULFILLMENT

Father God, I pray for my children, that they will trust in the Lord with all their hearts. May they not lean on their own understanding but grow to acknowledge God in all their ways so that you can direct their paths. I pray that they shall not be clueless as it relates to destiny matters. Cause them to gain the clarity and understanding the Spirit of God brings.

I pray Oh Lord that they will find a shepherd in you. I pray that they may always trust in your direction to lead them to their green pastures and still waters in

Jesus name. Lead him in the paths of righteousness for your namesake, that even though they walk through the struggles and pressures of this life, they will fear no evil but grow to understand that you are always with them to comfort, strengthen, and straighten them.

I declare that my children will grow to understand that you have prepared and set ready their portion of overflowing blessings, and to boldly take that which is theirs. Direct their steps, show them your ways, and teach them your paths oh Lord. Teach them to profit as you lead them on which way to go.

I declare that my children seek your wisdom daily knowing that you give to all who ask liberally and without reproach. I pray Lord that you will grant me the insight into the path you have designed for my child and help me to lead them right. I know you have a robust plan for their life's work and welfare.

I pray that you oh lord will make all things to align, function, operate, and produce well for my children because they are called according to your purpose. Just like Abraham, Moses, Joseph, David, Deborah, Mary, and many others in the bible who fulfilled their destiny, I pray that my children will fulfill their divine destiny in Jesus name. They shall not be nonentities, but they shall become noble, excellent, and significant men and women in the name of Jesus.

Like David, John the Baptist, Jesus, and Paul, I pray that my child will discern their assignment and purpose here on earth early and pursue its fulfillment. I pray that they will hear and obey God's law and delight to serve their generation according to the will of God.

Lord, I know there is a destiny you have in mind for these children you gave me, and I know this is what you want most for my children. I don't want them to settle for the glory and honor that the world offers. I want them to be crowned with the glory and honor that comes from you. As they are joined to Christ, cause them to take hold of the destiny you have in mind for all of them—ruling and reigning with you in a new heaven and new earth. I decree that they will live by God's principles. They will seek the Lord about what he wants and will do and say what the Lord tells them to as they are led in Jesus' name.

Scripture Reference: Psalms 23:1-6, Psalms 37:23, 119:133, 25:4,   Isaiah 48:17, 58:11, 32:8, Proverbs 3:5-6; 1 chronicles 10:13-14, James 1:5-8, Matt 7:7-8, Proverbs 16:9,   Jeremiah. 29:11, Rom. 12:2, Rom. 8:28, Psalms 25:9, Acts 13:36, Heb. 10:7

10. PRAYER FOR ACADEMIC EXCELLENCE

I declare that my children are the head and not the tail, they are above only and never beneath. I declare that they take a position in the forefront of all endeavors. They champion and pioneer ideas, insights, and concepts. They make the top in their classes. Like Daniel, they thrive in divine wisdom, possess skill in all learning, and express intelligence and understanding of the Holy Spirit. The Spirit of excellence is upon them and I see it manifest in their academics, social interactions, mental abilities, and spiritual prowess.

I declare that they are ten times better than their competitors. I declare that the life of God in their human spirit is the light and the development of their minds. They have an excellent spirit and a sound mind. They have supernatural intelligence in Jesus' name.

 I declare and I pray that my children be distinguished above all. I decree that they are more capable than their peers. They stand out spiritually, academically, and in their character. They have the knowledge and understanding to solve problems, create and provide solutions, innovate and float phenomenal ideas, insights, and concepts.

I decree that my children will be fruitful and they will excel above their average peers and that my children will be skillful in their work. I profess they are successful and stand before kings, noblemen, presidents, and industry giants, not ordinary, mere, and obscure men. Their gifts are making and creating room for them. I pray that they will develop self-leadership to do any school work, home duty, spiritual exercise placed before them readily and heartily. They will work at it hard and cheerfully.

I pray that you will divinely pick my children's teachers, nannies, caregivers, and lecturers. Give them teachers and tutors after your heart that will guide them in knowledge understanding. May they never be trapped in the care of witches, wizards, molesters, and wicked men and women in Jesus' name.

Scripture Reference: Daniel 1:17-20, Deuteronomy 28:13, Colossians 3:23-24, Proverbs 22:29, Daniel 6:3, 5:12

11. PRAYER FOR OBEDIENCE.

My children listen to their father's instruction and they do not forsake their mother's teachings and lessons. My children are wise to hear my instruction to them. I call them obedient children. They will wear my counsels like ornaments and it shall be well with them and they will gain many honors. They obey and honor me so it is well with them and they shall live long and prosper.

I declare and decree that my children are God's good and perfect gifts to me. They are the blessing of God and they shall not bring me sorrow but only rejoicing. They will bring me peace, pride, and fulfillment in my evening years. We declare that our children are not stubborn and rebellious in Jesus name.

 Lord, I pray that they will not cause me shame and bring me reproach. They will not ignore instruction or stray from the words of wisdom or knowledge they receive from us.

I pray for myself that I will take heed to guard my life diligently lest I forget the things which my eyes have seen and lest they depart from my mind and hearts so that I can teach them to my children and my children's children. I pray that my children will not become desensitized to sin and evil. I pray for them that every time they are faced with a decision to make, they will choose life over death. I pray that they will obey and serve God, so they shall spend their days in prosperity and their years in pleasure. I declare that they have an obedient heart, they respond to God and to me and so they eat the best of the Land. I declare that they obey the voice of God, He is their God and they are his people, they walk in all the way he commands them, so it is well with them. I declare that they hear the word of God and obey so they are blessed. As I use the rod of discipline when necessary it is driving foolishness far from them.

Father, I pray that my children will not be swallowed up by the world's mold.
   Scripture Reference: Proverbs 1:8-9, 10:22, 19:26-27, Colossians 3:20, James1:17, Deuteronomy. 4:9

12. PRAYER FOR WISDOM AND PERSONAL EXCELLENCE

I am a blessed daughter of the Most High God. I am in a covenant relationship with my father God through my union with Christ. I am happy, fortunate, and to be envied. I fear, revere, and worship God and delight greatly in his commandment so my child is equally blessed. I belong to the tribe of the Lion of Judah, so my children are Lions and Eagles. They are empowered and invested by Zoe to excel and exceed their natural abilities. They will go beyond the ordinary and be extraordinary, they are smarter than their equals, they surmount all obstacles, and they scale all barricades and barriers in Jesus' name. They shall not be small or mediocre, but they are of an excellent spirit. I declare that my best is their least and starting point. My seed manifest as first-class because they belong to the God-class.

My genealogy is blessed and enabled by divine favor and all spiritual blessing so I declare that my children (call their names) are mighty. That is, they are honored, celebrated, and distinguished everywhere they go. They grow in grace to influence their world for the kingdom. The seed of greatness, nobility, and prominence is resident in my child and it is finding expression all the time in Jesus name.

I decree that they are enabled to grow in wisdom, grace, and favor with God and men. They stand out all the time. I receive wisdom to instill, train and guide my child to choose the right path they should go in keeping with their gift, so that when they are old they will not depart from it. I will not provoke, stir, or incite my children to wrath or anger but I will bring them up in the training, counsel, guidance, and admonition of the Lord. Help me Father God, to administer the rod of discipline appropriately and on time.

Cause them to flourish like a well-nurtured plant, and may they be like a graceful pillar, carved to beautify a palace. May our family enjoy the satisfaction and security of having Jesus as our King! **Scripture Reference: Psalm 112:1-2[Amp], Luke 1:42, Prov. 22:6, Ephesians 6:4**

13. PRAYER FOR CONFIDENCE AND SECURITY

Lord, I pray for my children that their confidence will be rooted in who they are in Christ not based on their natural heritage and descent. I pray that they will not be deceived or discouraged by their physical features, status, achievements or even limitations. May they grow to understand who they truly are in Christ and to know they have a rich inheritance in God. I pray for them that God will open their eyes to see and their hearts to understand what He has freely provided for them in Christ.

I pray that they will focus on what matters to give them a right standing before God as against what matters to people. I pray that they shall not become men pleasers but God pleasers. They shall not be addicted to the approval of men, but be confident of who they are in God, what they have been divinely given and what they in turn can give. Father God, cause them to learn to judge their value by the value God has placed on them through the shed blood and sacrifice of Jesus, rather than the color of their skin, their height, features, or any human qualifications. I declare that they know and believe that they are fearfully and marvelously made! I declare that the good work God has started in them, will be brought to competition.

Father God, cause them to focus on adorning the inner man over the outward appearance and by so doing, become pleasing in the sight of God. I pray that my children will live in the true revelation of what it means to be a child of God. That they may fully understand their heavenly status in Christ and how it applies to them here on earth. I pray that they would understand that they have been blessed with all spiritual blessings in heavenly places. I declare that they are a chosen generation, a royal priesthood, a holy nation, God's special people, who proclaim His praises because He has brought them out of darkness into His marvelous light.

May they flourish like a well-nurtured plant and be like a graceful pillar, carved to beautify a palace. May our family enjoy the satisfaction and security of having Jesus as our King.
Scripture Reference: 1 Samuel 16:7, 1 Peter 3:3-4, Psalms 139:13-14, John 1:12, Ephesians 2:6, Romans 8:1, Deuteronomy 33:27, Philippians 1:6

14. PRAYER AGAINST SATANIC ATTACK

Father, you are the mighty one in battle, El-Shaddai! Contend with those who contend with my children. Fight against those who fight against me, through the attacks on my children. Deal with all satanic and demonic agents that might be a threat to their lives. Harass my harassers. Lord put on your armor, stand up for my help because you are my deliverer. Let your divine shield halt every arrow of the enemy directed against our children. Frustrate every plan of my enemies to defeat my children. Pursue and persecute them.

Let them be put to shame and dishonor who are against my children. Let them be turned back and confounded who plan our hurt and downfall. Let them be like chaff before the wind and let the Angel of the Lord drive them out. Let their ways be dark and slippery and let the Angel of the Lord afflict them. Let destruction befall them unawares. Let the trap they hid for us catch them and let them fall into the same trap.

I take authority over every plan, manipulation, and the maneuvers of demons, devils, and evil spirits against my children, and I overthrow all such. I cover my children with the blood of Jesus. Let the blood of Jesus protect them from evil friends in school, evil teachers, and all perpetrators of evil lurking around them. I bind these devils and drive them out in Jesus' Name! I declare that my children are far from the thought of oppression and destruction. Terror and fear are far from them. They shall not be tormented with fear or terror. It shall not come near them.

I resist any temptation of depression, discouragement, and despair attempting to creep into the lives of my children. They shall never be suicidal. People may gather against them, but not by God, Whosoever (man, woman, boy, girl) that shall gather together against them shall fall for their sake. They shall never be victims of kidnapping, physical and emotional abuse, neglect, sexual assault, rape, violation, molestation, accidents, evil conspiracies, negative peer pressures, pornography, etc. in Jesus' Name!

No evil shall befall them. There shall no sorcery, spell, divination, curse, or enchantment targeted at or directed at my children ever prevail, stand or succeed in Jesus Name. I neutralize, terminate, and annul them by the blood in Jesus' Name.

On behalf of my children, I take authority over all the power that the enemy possesses and no weapon formed against my children shall ever harm them. I trample upon serpents and scorpions and all the devil's physical, and mental strength and ability and nothing he attempts against my children shall prosper. My children's teeth shall not be set on edge because of any sour grapes I ate or because of the sins of their ancestors. They shall not be partakers of my sins and iniquities or the sins and iniquities of my parents, grandparents, or family, but rather they shall be recipients of God's mercy to thousands of generations down the line. I refuse and disallow that the Goliaths in my family should destroy my children. I disconnect them from bloodline demons and devils in Jesus name.

Scripture Reference: Isaiah 54;14-17, Numbers 23;23, James 4;7, Psalm 35;1-7, Luke 10;19, Ezekiel 18:2, Ex 20:5-6 Matthew 18;18

15. PRAYER FOR COURAGE

Lord, I pray for my children that they will know that fear has no place in their lives as Christians. May they grow to understand the authority they have been given in Christ over fear, to rebuke it in the name of Jesus. I ask that they will find peace from the Spirit of God to walk in his power, love, and self-discipline. I pray for them, that they will not be afraid of or terrified by any man, circumstance, or situation. As they live their lives according to the will of God, may they constantly be aware of the promise of His presence with them, which makes them bold and courageous. I pray that as the mountains surround Jerusalem so the presence of God will surround my children.

I pray that they will live fearless and emboldened by the strength of God no matter what is going on around them. Our Lord God increases their faith so that they can be firm in their belief. May they entrust their life into your hands knowing that you can take care of them better than we can.

I declare that my children are strong and courageous and that they shall not dread people or situations, knowing that the Lord God goes before them and that He will not leave them or forsake them.

I pray for my children that they have strength for all things in Christ who empowers them. They shall be ready for anything and equal to anything through Christ who infuses inner strength into them. They are self-sufficient in Christ's sufficiency. I pray that my children will grow to be strong and courageous. They shall not be afraid of men, nor be dismayed by situations and circumstances. I pray that God will be with them wherever they go like he was with Joshua.

I ask that my children will not fret or be anxious about anything. They will grow up to turn their concerns into conversations with God and their troubles into thanksgiving.
Scripture Reference: Psalms 56:3-4, Isaiah 41:10,13, Matthew 10:28, 1 Corinthians 16:13, Philippians 1:12-14, Deuteronomy 31:6, 1

Chronicles 28:20, Philippians 4:13, Joshua 1:8, Philippians 4:6

16. PRAYER FOR FAVOUR

Lord, I pray for my children to grow in grace, strength, wisdom, and favor with God and man. That you will bless and keep them and make your face to shine upon them and be gracious to them. Lift their countenance and give them peace continually.

Let them embrace mercy and truth so closely that they are highly esteemed before God and man. Surround my children with your favor and grace like a force field to attract good things and good people to them. Bring them into the favor and goodwill of family, friends, teachers, bosses, etc. At every juncture in their lives, arise and show them your mercy and favor. Like Noah, let them find grace in your eyes oh Lord.

Guide them continually and satisfy their soul. Strengthen their bones; let them be like a watered garden and like a spring of water whose waters do not fail.

I pray that the beauty of the Lord will be upon them, and establish the work of their hands. Grant them good understanding in all areas of life that they may

gain favor. May the sons of foreigners build up their walls and kings minister to them.
Scripture Reference: Numbers 6:24-26, Proverbs 3:1-4, 13:15, Psalms 5:12, Daniel 1:9, Genesis 6:8, Psalms 102:13, 1 Samuel 2:26, Isaiah 58:11, 60:10, Psalms 90:17

17. PRAYER FOR LEADERSHIP AND INFLUENCE

My seed shall be mighty (honored, celebrated, and distinguished) everywhere they go because my spiritual heritage is blessed. The seed of greatness is in my child and it is finding expression all the time.

My children are fruitful; they are capable and productive and every effort they put into life will yield great dividends for them. They shall produce effective, efficient, and excellent results in Jesus' name. Their lives will not reflect barrenness in Jesus' name. They multiply and they fill the earth. They greatly increase in capacity and output. My children are

Multi-talented. They enlarge and expand in thinking and expression daily. They gain increase as they grow. They replenish and nourish the earth, they subdue the earth and they take dominion.

They conquer and surmount all things that oppose

their progress and well-being. They prevail over life's battles and they triumph in victory all the time. They are not brought down and defeated but they win always! They are resilient and do not give up easily. My children exceed, excel, succeed, and flourish in life. They eclipse all doubts, fear and unbelief, and all limitations. They exercise their authority and influence over creation. They ascend and reign in this life as kings.

I declare and pray that my children are the light of the world. I call them a city set on a hill that cannot be hidden. They are bold and brilliant. I call them prominent, eminent, and remarkable. The spirit of leadership is in them. They carry the mantle to take the lead in their pursuits. They shall not be obscure or nameless. My children make an impressive impact on their world. They shall leave indelible footprints in their times.

I declare and pray that my children are shielded from the pollutions of the world's puny, negative, and limiting thought patterns. Their minds are ruled by divine counsel. They function in godly wisdom. They are shaped and sharpened by divine insights and understanding.

I declare and pray that my children dwell on whatever is true, honorable, just, pure, lovely, and is commendable and admirable.

Scripture Reference: Matthew 5:13-16, 20:26, 1 Timothy 3:2, Romans 12:8, Genesis 1:28, Proverbs 4:23

18. RELATIONSHIP, MARRIAGE, AND PURITY

I pray that my children will hold a higher standard than the world. They shall be approved as excellent, pure, and blameless in character and conduct. Lord, I can't protect them from every temptation, and I can't instill in them a resolve not to sin when temptation comes after them. Only you can protect from the enemy that seeks to rob, kill, and destroy. Only you can instill in them a desire to please you that is greater than their desire to please themselves. Give them clarity about the wickedness of sexual sin. Give them resolve to live a pure life. And fill them with a growing love for you that would make it more and more unthinkable to sin against you.

Father, I need wisdom from you to know how to guide them toward purity in a world of available sexual images, aggressive sex peddlers, and acceptance of sexual perversion. Give me the wisdom to recognize my own need for your power to overcome sexual temptation and words to express the availability of forgiveness and cleansing for sexual sinners. Help my children become sensitized to sin and evil. Father, I pray that my children will not be swallowed up by the world's mold.

Lord, I pray for my children to be connected to the right persons in life even as they are groomed to be the right people. When he or she is old enough to get married order his or her steps to your choice son or daughter ordained for them. May they hear your voice and follow after your guidance to that person that is right for them; and they shall not make wrong choices. I disconnect them from unbelieving, carnal, dishonest, disorderly, and dysfunctional men and women.

I pray that my children shall grow in the conviction of truth on purity. I pray that they will present and dedicate their bodies to you in consecration and holiness knowing that marriage is honorable and the bed is undefiled.

I pray for my children, that they will not experience marital delays. Their marriages will be founded on Christ's relationship with the church. I pray for them that they will build healthy happy homes as a witness of the Holy Union of Christ and His church. **Scripture Reference: Philippians 1:9-10, Genesis 2:18, Hebrews 13:4, John10:10,1 Corinthians 6:18, 1 Corinthians 7:2, Proverbs 18:22, Proverbs 19:14**

CREATING SYNERGY THROUGH THE MUM'S PRAYER CIRCLE VISION

"Two are better than one because they have a good reward for their labour, for if they fall , one will lift up his companion. But woe to him who is alone when he falls, for he has no one to help him up. "Ecclesiastes 4:9-10

It can be somewhat difficult to pray alone. Sometimes we get discouraged and distressed because we are tired, overwhelmed, or burdened. This can easily make us give up on the whole practice of prayer. A good place to find refuge and support in your times of weakness will be a prayer circle or group comprising of a few mothers like you.

It is easier to stand together than to stand alone.

You can create or join an existing mums' prayer group for all the support you will need. This group will also serve as an accountability group. We need mums to encourage each other and to challenge each other to do the right things. You can remind each other of your commitment to pray for your children continuously and follow up on each other. You can schedule weekly prayer times together to keep the flow.

You can share prayer points and stand in faith with another mum to strengthen and multiply power so as to ensure that your prayer is answered. A burden shared can be a great relief and that enables a mum to go through the emotional pressures of their role with greater ease, knowing she is not alone in the situation.

This group will serve as a place where you can share testimonies of answered prayers and challenge each other to good works. The Bible admonishes that we should rejoice with those that rejoice and to share in their joy. You are light: shine your light wherever you find yourself. Don't hide under the bushel. Start a Mums prayer circle today.

CATALYZE

CHAPTER NINE

GOD'S WAITING ROOM

This book will be incomplete without dropping a word of hope and faith for every woman who is waiting on God for a baby. I am a woman, and I've been a biological sister to one who was in the waiting room for 10 years before her breakthrough came. As Pastor for over two decades, I have had to pray, cry, believe, and wait with many women. So believe me when I say, "I share in the pain, agony, and disappointment which comes with delayed conception or losing a child at Pre-Term or at birth." Yes, I call it delayed conception because that is just what it is! God promised children to everyone. The command to be fruitful is to all humanity, and to the believer in Christ He says, "…none shall be barren in the land."

"Then God blessed them, and God said to them, "Be fruitful and multiply; fill the earth and subdue it; have dominion over the fish of the sea, over the birds of the air, and over every

living thing that moves on the earth." Genesis 1:28

Do you see! Bareness and delayed conception are satanic disruptions resulting from the fall. In scripture, we see that fruitfulness is your fundamental human right. God wants you to have children. The devil cannot give you a child; and even when it appears that he does, he uses the distress of women seeking the fruit of the womb to web them into dangerous covenants that create heartbreaking consequences. Remember it is only the blessings of God that make rich and adds no sorrow.

"The blessing of the Lord makes one rich, And He adds no sorrow with it." Proverbs 10:22

But the seeming blessing of the devil will bring plenty of sorrow. Wait for God! I know it's not easy and funny to wait. Waiting can be the hardest thing ever to do, but with your faith in God and heavens help you shall prevail. God also promised that His people will be fruitful in the covenant.

"Ye shall serve the Lord your God, and......there shall nothing cast their young nor be barren." Exodus 23:26

But after the fall, notwithstanding the obstruction

from Satan, God made a robust provision for fruitfulness in the new covenant to which you and I belong, and this one surpasses the old covenant.

"But now has he obtained a more excellent ministry by how much also he is the mediator of a better covenant, which was established upon better promises." Hebrews 8:6

If the old covenant which was faulty and sealed with the blood of animals delivered value, how much more the new covenant which was sealed by the blood of Jesus. Will it not provide much more value? There is no biological defect in your body or your spouse's that God cannot heal based on the fact that Jesus already took your infirmities, and bore your sicknesses on the cross of Calvary.

"And Jesus looking upon them saith, with men it is impossible, but not with God all things: for with God all things are possible." Mark 10:27

The Bible records numerous testimonies of how God intervened in the life of women who were unable to have children immediately after marriage. There was only one woman who remained without a child till death, and that was because she despised God. Her name was Micah, David's wife. Women such as Sarah (Genesis 11:30), Rebekah, Isaac's wife (Gen

25:21), Rachel, one of Jacob's wives (Genesis 29-31), Manoah's nameless wife, Samson's mother (Judges 13:2), Hannah (1 Samuel 1:1-5), Elizabeth (Luke 1:7) all eventually had babies.

Each of these women listed above later became pregnant with God's help, and interestingly all the resulting babies were boys. God remembered each of these women at a point in time. I declare concerning you in the name of Jesus, God will remember you also! God has not forsaken you. It may seem so, but His delay most times is so that he can demonstrate His power and have all men worship Him.

It is usually not easy on a woman's emotion when she is waiting. She might begin to feel less than a woman, because of the family and societal pressures. This can weigh her down especially if she doesn't have a strong support system like strong faith in God, a supportive husband, or family. Women go through a lot of pain and humiliation in such cases. All sorts of accusing fingers are pointed at her. In certain cultures, she is blamed for the delay. Her husband may hardly come under any pressure for being the cause of infertility, except maybe from family members who might be asking him to find an alternative wife. At this point, people forget it is God who opens the womb not man. Believe me, *even when a woman is medically*

assisted to conceive, it is a miracle!

My dear sister who is waiting on God, do not be dismayed. Let not your heart be troubled, for this Egyptian you see today you will see them no more. The Lord God is mindful of you and He has a plan. It might seem to be taking forever, but God's promises are true and cannot fail. ***"For with God nothing is ever impossible and no word from God shall be without power or impossible of fulfillment." (Amplified) Luke 1:37***

Hold on to the promises of God until it becomes your reality. I spotted a few stories from women like you who had to wait for children. Perhaps you can relate to these, and the Lord will use their stories to uplift you, strengthen you, and bring your hope alive again. These are real-life stories of women who are willing to reveal their identities and use their stories to encourage every other woman presently in God's waiting room.

PASTOR ONYEMA MONYE'S TESTIMONY.

I got married in March 1997 and was not planning to have children immediately, but in the next couple of months, I and my husband decided to try having children. By the end of 1997 - 9 months after - we didn't see any results. So in the next one year - 1998, I started getting a little bit anxious, and then we further agreed to go to the hospital. On getting to the hospital, we discovered that we both had issues. While mine was related to my fallopian tubes, my husband's issue was related to his sperm count. And by then, the doctors mentioned there was no guarantee that I may bear children and that it would only take a miracle. Although the doctors prescribed drugs for my husband, according to their report, medically there was a very low chance that I would take in, and the fact that IVF (In-vitro Fertilization) was not popular at that time, making it difficult to rely on a medical solution.

At this point, my faith was not challenged because my husband and I resolved to go to God, the Giver of children. We were not devastated and we still had hope in God. So we decided to stay with God, to trust and stand upon His word. Although there was not any form of direct pressure, during the third year of our waiting, there was a subtle pressure to see a gynecologist. There was also indirect pressure especially when attending a friend's baby dedications. In all of these, we still stayed with God's word trusting and waiting on Him. During this whole experience of waiting, some of the things that played major roles aside from prayers were the word of God and faith. I was more particular about working on my faith level, by bringing my faith to the point of receiving from God. Although I like to pray, I don't think I was spending hours or days fasting and praying to have children. I was, however, studying the word of God, learning the principles of faith, applying these principles of faith, trusting God for children. I would meditate on His word until I gained understanding, and then I would make declarations. It was a fight of faith for me as there was a point when I decided to go through a certain process to achieve what I was trusting God for.

My turning point was when I heard this statement that was made in the church: "If you say you know something and there's no proof of it, then you don't know it!" I was challenged by that statement and then decided to study the Bible from book to book, beginning from Genesis, believing that by the time I get to Revelation, I would receive my light and receive my breakthrough. So I started working on my faith level by studying the word of God, listening to messages, and going to Bible School. I enrolled at Word of Faith Bible Institute (WOFBI) for a month and read books, some of which were written by Bishop David Oyedepo like: ***"You Shall Not be Barren", "Supernatural Childbirth" and "The Force of Faith".***

In building my faith level, I also held on to Hebrews 11, meditating on the power of faith, how faith works, and how it operates. I believed that with faith, I can do anything and by faith, I can get my breakthrough. For me, it was also understanding the meaning of faith, the different principles and components of faith, and how to work it out in my life. I also studied the life of Abraham relying on my favorite scripture - *Romans 4* where it mentioned that "Abraham was fully convinced!" That was the scripture I stood upon as I kept working at it until I got to a point where I could truly tell myself that I was fully persuaded, fully assured, and fully convinced about what God has promised. This was the litmus test for me as I would measure my faith based on this scripture, I aimed to get to a faith level where I could truly say, my faith was absolute.

It eventually came to a point where I was at the level of great faith, and then I knew at that point I couldn't be denied what I was trusting God for. It was shortly after that, four years after my wedding, that I got pregnant and had my first baby. Then came my second, the third and then the fourth! I had four pregnancies altogether, all in quick succession without any further delays. Praise God!

So, for every woman who is waiting, you may need to

approach your waiting as though you are managing a project. As in project management where you need to be intentional and deliberate in your goals and actions in order to achieve the desired result. You may also want to apply the same principles that worked for me as you wait. With this, you'd have to begin to tell yourself the truth as to whether or not you are backing your faith with works, such as declarations and confessions of the word, studying the scriptures, reading of books, etc.

Being that you have the desired result in sight, you'd be able to measure and control your actions to be sure they are still in line with God's word about you. Again, just like in project management, you begin to see that there's a time-frame to this, there is a beginning date and an ending date. So just keep trusting and believing God for a miracle, and as the word of God says, "...surely there's an end and the expectations of the righteous shall not be cut short." From the beginning of your waiting on God, look unto Him as your source. You must come to a point where you first believe in the ability of God to give you your breakthrough. So focus on God and remove every other option. Don't be counting on God and still be thinking of options. Fully concentrate on God, let Him lead you as you put all your hope and trust in Him.

MRS VICTORIA OMALE'S TESTIMONY

Before I got married in 2005, I discovered my period had stopped the previous year before my wedding, but I was very naïve and didn't see it as anything. Even when my husband noticed and brought my attention to the fact that I never carried a sanitary pad, I still didn't see it as a big deal. But then again, maybe because we were not planning to have children yet, so there wasn't any cause for alarm. But in the next few months, we decided to start having babies. It was then we realized that my period wasn't coming, and no pregnancies as well. So I went to the hospital to run some scans. That was when I found out that I had *polycystic variance syndrome* – a hormonal imbalance, and with this, it was clear that my ovaries were not developing eggs to a certain maturity point to conceive. Although, even when the doctor mentioned that due to the fact that it was less than one year since we got married, there wasn't a big deal. He said that they were going to look for ways to enable my system. I knew at that point that pregnancy may be a challenge. I was still a little bit unconcerned because even in the scriptures, I couldn't remember any woman who was barren except one person.

However, anxiety started to increase after that entire year passed, so, I went to see another gynecologist who also confirmed the initial diagnosis. I was placed on some medications and injections which eventually would mess up my system. This medication would make me feel pregnant; and when the time comes, I'd bleed and feel I had a miscarriage. It was at this point, I had a run play with my emotions, as getting pregnant began to look like an uphill task. In June 2006, however, I got pregnant, (although I had not seen my period) but I lost my baby. September of that same year, it happened again, which marked the beginning of a roller-coaster experience for me. All the injections I was being given seemed to be failing even when this same treatment gave other people multiple babies. I was just blowing up and adding a lot of weight and this was really scary for me.

I became a lab rat with these treatments, so I had to stop as it became too much, I needed to rest my system. This situation challenged my faith as I would describe myself as a lover of Jesus, but wasn't seeing any tangible proof in this regard of pregnancy. I would be like, God; "I've served you, have led people to you, did everything, I'm supposed to be a testimony. This was supposed to be a smooth sail; where's that part of me? The glory is not there, what am I saying? What am I doing? What am I glorifying?" There were days, I would walk around my estate, would shed tears, and then clean my eyes and head back home. At some points, I even compared myself to a friend who was then pregnant at that same time with me, but had her own baby. The good thing was when all these were happening, I held on to a word I had received in 2004 while I was in school even before I got married.

While I was in fellowship, a word of knowledge came at a time from the Man of God that "There is somebody, whose period has stopped and you are concerned, God said you are going to have children and the first would be a boy." This was what I held unto, years after year. That was really my anchor word even though my mind was then crowded with other things happening. In all of these, I would still pray, go around and travel to churches, attend night vigils, make sacrifices, pledges, and I would fast.

Prior to receiving a scripture and before my second miscarriage, I got used to the fact that once I get pregnant, I would lose it. The thought of blood would automatically hit me. I stopped peeing at the toilet and started sitting at the bathtub, expecting to see blood and when the second pregnancy came, I lost it, lost the third and fourth as well. When I took in for the fourth pregnancy, I had a dream. In that dream, I walked into Bishop Abioye's office and there was a couple with him in his office. The moment I walked in with my husband, he got up from his chair, laid one hand on my head and the other on my stomach, then he said it is done in the Name of Jesus and I said Amen! Then I woke up. But, about four weeks later, when it was confirmed that I was pregnant for the fourth one, I lost it again.

It was after this occurrence, I had to learn to fight for myself because God had spoken in different ways. At this point, I knew it was important to fight for myself in the place of prayer and faith. It was after this resolve that the understanding of the word now came, and I got the insight that I needed to apply the word in my life. I held on to Exodus 23:25, consistently declaring the fact that "I will not miscarry, I will not cast my young."

In 2011, when I went to the hospital, the doctor placed me again on the previous medication and injections I was on before, but this time around I would reinforce this by declaring the word of God that I will not cast my young. I was then confirmed pregnant again. The doctor told me to ponder like Mary, keep it in my heart and that was what I did because all the previous pregnancies didn't scale past three months. I decided to engage in warfare on this particular pregnancy. Whenever I start to expect blood, I would declare and say: "Satan, the Lord rebuke you, over my life, over my baby, the Lord rebuke you! I will not cast my young, I will not miscarry!" I even stopped sitting in the bathtub and even when I started seeing blood this time around, the baby stayed, it was past three months and eventually, I had my baby - my first child (a baby boy) after seven years of waiting!

I had my first baby in January 2012, eight months later in September 2012, my period came back on its own – the first time since 2004! I later took in again and had my second son in June 2013; and after that as the babies started coming, I just started losing all the weight. Now, as I look back, I must mention the fact that I experienced a lot of pressure both directly and indirectly. I even had cruel comments like people wondering if I was a man or a woman; some wondered if I was happy for others who had gotten their babies. I experienced all sorts of humiliating treatments. Some people even thought I bought my first child, and they wanted to see evidence by observing me to see if my child would feed on my breast! But I have had the last laugh, because God gave me more than one child. The evidence is clear! Today, I'm glad God answered all those remarks by granting me the fruits of the womb.

MY REMARKS:

For every woman waiting, there's nothing that is impossible with God. I've come to experience it. It can be very difficult when you're going through it, but what's most important is for you to hold on to God. The waiting period is not forever! It can be 10 years, it can be 15 years but they don't always last forever. If God has promised you, He will do it, that's just the bottom line.

Glory to God! I am reminded of the scripture in Hebrews 6:12, "That ye be not slothful, but followers of them who through faith and patience inherit the promises." Hmmnn, Children are from God, the fruit of the womb is his reward. You might have a delay, but it is not a denial. Through your life and testimony, others will receive their blessing. I remember one of the testifiers sharing with me how other women have conceived as well just by sharing her story with them. Weep no longer daughter of the highest, for your salvation, has come.

I declare that you are blessed among women and blessed is the fruit of your womb!

I call you the mother of children and fruitful vine!

I declare and decree that your children are like olive plants round about your table!

Halleluyah!

RESOURCES

Nancy, Guthrie. The one year praying through the bible for your kids. Carol Stream, IL:Tyndale House Publishers,2016

Marina, Basta, Brody.J.Lipsett. Anatomy, Abdomen and Pelvis Umblical Cord. Treasure Island , FL: Stats Pearls Publishing, 2020

Lisa Roundy, The impact of mother's emotional and Physical state on the prenatal Environment. Accessed February 2, 2020, https//study.com?academy/lesson

Robert Malone, Scientist discover Children's cell living in mother's brains.Accessed February 2, 2020, Scientificamerican.com

U.   S Department of Education, Early childhood (birth to Eight Years) middle childhood (Eight to Twelve Years). Accessed February 3, 2020, https://educationstateuniversity.com/pages/1826/

Stages of Development of Psychology of People at different ages from infancy to old age. PsychologyDiscussion.net

Start a
MUMS PRAYER CIRCLE

today in your neighbourhood
or join one around you.

Join our Facebook group, **(Mothers on a Mission Supplication Group)** a community of purposeful and like-minded mothers and aspiring mums who provide prayer support, inspiration and motivation to empower each other on this path.

Follow me on Facebook and on Instagram **@xceptionalfranca.**

visit
www.francaatokolo.com
for other resources.

Email: francaatokolo@gmail.com
or call: +2348127556388